# Islamic
# Architecture

ERIC BROUG

# Islamic Architecture

## A WORLD HISTORY

# Contents

## 1   EASTERN MEDITERRANEAN & GULF REGION

## 2   IRAQ, IRAN & SOUTH ASIA

## 3   TURKEY & CENTRAL ASIA

PAGE 2

**ORBELIANI BATHHOUSE, TBILISI, GEORGIA** (18TH C)
Tbilisi, the capital of Georgia, is famed for its hot sulphur springs. It is thought that in the 13th century there were over sixty bathhouses; now there are fewer than ten, of which the Orbeliani bathhouse is the most ornate and eyecatching. With its large recessed pointed arch and glazed ceramic tiles, it recalls Persian architecture. It attracted famous visitors, including authors Alexandre Dumas and Alexander Pushkin.

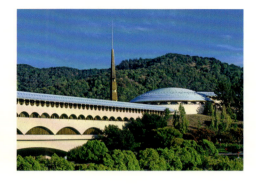

# 4 AFRICA

# 5 ASIA PACIFIC

# 6 EUROPE & THE AMERICAS

# Introduction

'If you want to know about us,
examine our buildings.'

INSCRIPTION ON A TIMURID BUILDING IN SAMARKAND

When we think of Islamic architecture, it typically brings to mind a few key monuments and regions. The important buildings tend to dominate our understanding of a place or a period. Mosques with huge domes and pencil-thin minarets characterize the Ottoman style; colourful ceramic geometric compositions decorate the Marinid architecture of Fes and Marrakech in Morocco. Over the decades a narrative has developed in academic research that anything of interest in Islamic architecture happened in the Middle East, North Africa, Central Asia, Turkey, India, Iraq, Iran and Afghanistan; and furthermore, that everything of interest was finished well before the 19th century. This, of course, is far from true, as this book will show. Islam is a global religion. There are more than three million mosques in the world, and it would be hard to find a single country in which there is not a building that either serves a Muslim community or has been influenced by Islamic architecture. Indeed, the term 'Islamic architecture' itself is not always a comfortable one. It can seem to suggest that a unifying religious component is always important and present. 'Architecture from Muslim societies' is probably a more accurate term.

The aim of this book is to present a selection of buildings that show this immense global richness and diversity. In these choices, I have been guided by beauty, visual interest and relevance: I have given myself permission *not* to choose buildings based solely

**GREAT MOSQUE OF BOBO DIOULASSO, BURKINA FASO** (EARLY TO MID-19TH C) Built of whitewashed mud brick, the mosque has a large open courtyard, a tower indicating the qibla and mihrab, and a minaret on the opposite side. Characteristic of the region's architecture are the wooden protruding beams, called *toron*, which serve as a sort of permanent scaffolding, enabling maintenance.

or principally on their historical importance. Fortunately, some of the most beautiful buildings are also historically important, so the Umayyad Mosque in Damascus (see pp. 10 and 40), the Dome of the Rock in Jerusalem (see pp. 12 and 47), the Alhambra in Granada (see pp. 256–59) and others are of course featured here. I have sought to show not only the finest buildings, but also some unfamiliar details of well-known buildings.

As with any selection, the challenge is not 'what do I include?' but 'what do I leave out?' It is impossible to create a book that defines the richness of architecture in all Muslim societies without some difficult selection decisions. Eventually, it became clear that I would inevitably make subjective choices, exercising more freedom but also more responsibility, and accepting that it would be impossible to please everybody, both in what is included and what is not.

This has been an immense educational journey for me. Having a master's degree in the history of Islamic architecture from SOAS in London, I thought I already knew quite a bit before I started work on this book, yet there turned out to be a huge amount that was new to me. For example, I was amazed to discover the wonderful adobe mosques of the northern Ivory Coast (see p. 204). Not only has this journey of discovery been humbling, it has shown how much about Islamic architecture is not yet being researched or documented.

Historians generally prefer to write about pivotal buildings and eras, or about earlier findings, reinforcing a focus on particular buildings and eras. So, if you want to know more about the Timurid architecture of Samarkand or the Mamluk architecture of Egypt, the main challenge is to decide what to read first. Conversely, if you want to learn about the architecture of the Sokoto Caliphate in West Africa or Tatar mosques in Russia, you may struggle to find very much at all. Research and documentation on architecture in Muslim societies is very uneven.

This book seeks to correct that imbalance, even if only in a small way, by presenting amazing buildings from around the globe, including several that have rarely, if ever, been featured in photographic books. There is still a long way to go. I myself am also a product of this educational bias and it has been hard not to fill the book with many of the numerous architectural highlights of the Timurid and Mamluk dynasties, or the Ottoman Empire.

Articles on Islamic architecture may describe in great detail how a building looks, and how it might resemble another building. I am indebted to those articles and their authors; without them I would not have been able to write this book. I have included a reference section of many of the articles and books that I benefited from in preparing this book, and which should provide numerous directions for further reading (see pp. 325–27).

Women are notably underrepresented in the history of the architecture of Muslim societies, although they sometimes played an important and independent role in the commissioning of buildings, and I have tried to touch on this subject (see pp. 312–19). With their greater access to mosque interiors, it is perhaps inevitable that most of the photographs in this book were taken by men, but the amazing cover image was taken by a female photographer from Egypt.

I have devoted my adult life to Islamic visual culture, mostly focusing on pattern and detail. I am fascinated by the art of making, by the skill and effort that men and women can devote to creating something beautiful, to make something more wonderful than is functionally necessary. Nowhere is this more in evidence, in my estimation, than in Islamic art and architecture, where beauty exists to honour Allah. I marvel at the ingenuity of the visual ideas in Islamic art and architecture, and the skills involved in executing them to very high standards. It is often asserted that craftsmen in Islamic societies were anonymous but, to my joy, I have sometimes been able to find names of builders, masons, carpenters, plaster carvers and others. Every building in this book was made by human hands, usually by men who had families to support, and in some cases by those who were labouring under duress, but who nonetheless understood that their professional responsibility was to make the best work. This ethos did not end before the 19th century; it continues today, and the evidence is in the pages that follow.

What has made this book possible only now is that there are many more high-quality photographs available from previously under-documented parts of the world, many of which are becoming available in online databases. It is now possible to find photographs of previously hard-to-find architecture in Niger or Somalia, or of a small community mosque in Bangladesh. Whereas in the past, a European photographer might fly to Uzbekistan for a week or two and take photos of all the 'exotic' architecture, now many places are captured by professional local photographers. They bring a different perspective and they can afford to take the time to go to out-of-the-way locations. Without the skills of these local photographers, this book would not exist.

Architecture is a unique way to engage with cultures other than our own. You can imagine walking through the doorway of, for example, a mosque in Dogon country in Mali (see p. 194) because it is a doorway like any other. As humans, we can understand that; it doesn't need to be explained to us. It makes it easier for us to relate to the building, and to imagine the environment in which it was created. This is why I have let the images in the book do most of the talking. What I ask of the reader is only to have a good look. I have studied at least half a million photos for this book to select the most visually eloquent from the widest possible range of sources, following a journey not just around the world but back in time through history. These images tell a story.

I grew up in the Netherlands, a pluralist society where tolerance is considered a national virtue. I have included subjects based on the criteria of relevance, beauty and visual interest, nothing else. I have cast my net as wide as possible, including buildings that are *influenced* by Islamic architecture, of which there are many. So, in addition to mosques, madrasas and other specifically Islamic buildings, you will find churches, synagogues, bathhouses, town halls and much else, whether sacred or secular. I have included Mozarab architecture (built by Christians living under Muslim rule in Spain), and Mudejar architecture (built by Muslims living under Christian rule in Iberia and South America), since they too are all part of the story of Islamic architecture. Of the countless awe-inspiring Ottoman mosques or Great Seljuk minarets that might deserve inclusion, I have chosen only two truly wonderful Ottoman mosques and one Great Seljuk minaret to stand for the many I left out, but thereby left space to show other things. In the same spirit, I have limited the number of photographs of the Topkapı Palace, partly because there are other books that show more, but mostly because I am eager to use these pages to share images of less well-known buildings that have the power to amaze and inspire us, and to provide an opportunity to consider Islamic architecture in a much wider context.

\* \* \*

After I had completed my first book, *Islamic Geometric Patterns*, I thanked God for his grace and for enabling me to write this book. I thought that was it; God's plan fulfilled. But then I was given the opportunity to write two more books on the same subject, much to my amazement. Again I thought, surely this is God's plan for me fulfilled. Now, I have written this book and I make no more claims to know what His plan is for me. I am humbled and grateful that this task fell to me.

# 1

# Eastern Mediterranean & Gulf Region

**UMAYYAD MOSQUE, DAMASCUS, SYRIA** (c. 715 CE)
Commissioned by the sixth caliph, al-Walid I, the Umayyad Mosque (sometimes known as the Great Mosque of Damascus) was built by very large numbers of labourers of different backgrounds, including Copts, Persians, North Africans, Greeks and Indians. Originally, all the façades of its courtyard would have been covered in gold leaf and glass mosaics, as well as the interior walls and undersides of arches. The mosaic compositions show natural landscapes and features, some recognizable and depicting heavenly landscapes with orchards. The splendour of the mosque and its architectural decoration became the benchmark against which all other mosques were measured.

Islamic architecture started with the Umayyad caliphate in Syria (661–750 CE). They built the Dome of the Rock in Jerusalem (see pp. 12 and 47) and the Umayyad Mosque in Damascus (see opposite and p. 40), but also many exceptionally interesting and beautiful palaces and castles, mostly in what is now Jordan. These buildings demonstrate that a new visual tradition does not start in a vacuum and also challenge what we consider to be typical of Islamic art. Eighth-century Qusayr Amra in Jordan (see p. 16) has many frescoes reflecting its purpose as a residential and agricultural complex, with images of craftsmen at work, dancing women, even a bear playing the guitar. It has the first known depiction of the sky on a dome interior, showing the constellations and the zodiac. Khirbat al-Mafjar in Jericho, also known as Hisham's Palace, shows that the curvilinear interlacing bands that characterize Roman and Byzantine mosaics are, in the new Umayyad context, also used to give geometry a starring role, rather than the traditional supporting role (see p. 46). It is probably the starting point of Islamic geometric design. The first horseshoe and pointed arches appear during the Umayyad era; the earliest pointed arch can be found in the circular colonnade inside the Dome of the Rock.

Islamic architecture in the Eastern Mediterranean region has given us many innovations and remarkable buildings. It can also remind us of the ways in which political factors and architecture are entwined. The Fatimids originated in North Africa, founding their capital, Mahdia, in Tunisia; but they ended up establishing the new city of Cairo (al-Qahirah) as the capital of their caliphate.

The Umayyads ruled only relatively briefly from Damascus; they were thrown out by the Abbasids, and those who survived fled to Córdoba, Spain, where they established a new empire. The Mamluks, who were responsible for dozens, if not hundreds, of exceptional buildings in Cairo, were initially military slaves from Central Asia, who deposed their masters and took over for themselves. Their mosques, madrasas and mausolea in Cairo show great attention to detail in stone carving, an innovative and bold approach to geometric design and a general commitment to quality. But the Mamluks' political culture was volatile: in the 267 years of Mamluk rule (1250–1517), there were almost fifty sultans. Many ruled for barely a year. Some were deposed but came back. Commissioning splendid buildings is often a way to claim legitimacy, either to the clergy or to the populace, especially if they are more splendid than your predecessors' or rivals' buildings. A good example of this

OPPOSITE
**AYYUBID: MAUSOLEUM OF IMAM AL-SHAFI'I, CAIRO, EGYPT** (1211)
For over a thousand years, this has been the most venerated shrine in Cairo. Imam al-Shafi'i is counted as one of the four great Sunni imams; the other three are Hanifa, Malik and Hanbal. Saladin founded a madrasa nearby dedicated to the Shafi'i school of jurisprudence and commissioned a marvellous wooden teak cenotaph, carved by Ubayd al-Najjar ibn Ma'ali in 1178/79, to be placed over the imam's grave. The mausoleum was built thirty years later.

BELOW
**UMAYYAD: DOME OF THE ROCK (QUBBAT AL-SAKHRA), JERUSALEM** (691 CE)
Built by Caliph Abd al-Malik, it is the earliest surviving Islamic monument. The rock inside (see p. 47) is believed to be the place from which Muhammad ascended to the heavens, and it is also said to be where Abraham was prepared to sacrifice his son Isaac. The interior is covered in exquisite golden mosaics. The exterior is now covered in 16th-century Ottoman-era tiles, but was originally clad in marble and mosaics, similar to the interior.

architectural one-upmanship can be seen with the three minarets of Cairo's al-Azhar Mosque (see p. 29).

In many ways, this chapter covers the epicentre of Islamic history and architecture: Damascus, Cairo and Mecca all appear here. The historical importance and marvellous nature of much of the Islamic architecture in Syria, Jordan, Palestine and Egypt means that the rest of the region typically receives less attention. Unjustly so, as shown by, for example, the plaster mihrabs of some Omani mosques – al-Shawadna mosque (see p. 55) is one of the best examples; the presence of a Chinese ceramic plate in the centre of its mihrab also tells a story about trade connections and cultural influence. In Yemen, there was a period of almost a hundred years when Queen Asma and her daughter-in-law, Queen Arwa, ruled over the Sulayhid empire: Queen Arwa's mosque in Jibla (see p. 59) is one of Yemen's oldest mosques. Yemen is also home to the wonderfully and painstakingly restored 16th-century al-Amiriya Madrasa (see p. 56), a decades-long labour of love for an Iraqi archaeologist and her huge team of craftspeople and builders.

In recent decades, the architecture of the countries in the Gulf region has given the world examples of excellence of design, and a boldness of vision that fits in with the centuries-old practice of rulers in Islamic history commissioning the biggest and best buildings, using the best builders and architects. Sometimes it is the details that are most telling. The Sultan Qaboos Grand Mosque in Oman (see p. 55) is much photographed, but I have chosen to focus on a small detail, something that might catch your eye if you were visiting. Similarly, the Beit al Quran museum in Bahrain (see pp. 52–53) has an astonishing stained-glass window that would demand your attention if you were there. Not everything that is built as contemporary architecture in the Gulf region can of course be considered 'Islamic architecture', but it is fascinating to see design elements of Islamic architecture interpreted for the 21st century in many of these projects. The Louvre museum in Abu Dhabi, UAE (see p. 23), filters light through the layering of a simple geometric design. The modernist Flying Saucer building in Sharjah, UAE (see p. 22), is evidently inspired by a star pattern from Islamic geometric design. One of the biggest challenges in this book was what to choose in Saudi Arabia. It would be inconceivable to create a book on Islamic architecture without a picture of the Kaaba, so it was especially gratifying to find a photo that shows a different perspective on pilgrims and their proximity to, and relationship with, the Kaaba.

**KAPSARC MUSALLA, RIYADH, SAUDI ARABIA** (2017)

Designed by Zaha Hadid, the campus of KAPSARC (King Abdullah Petroleum Studies and Research Center) in Saudi Arabia's capital is created as a modular structure that can grow over time. The angular, multifaceted white buildings hold together like a randomized honeycomb. The *musalla* (prayer space) is one of the initial five buildings. The campus is shielded from the southern sun but open to the north and west. Integrated windcatchers cool the courtyards and tunnels connect the buildings.

**UMAYYAD: MSHATTA, EASTERN DESERT, JORDAN** (743–744 CE)

This winter palace in the desert of Jordan was commissioned by Umayyad caliph Walid II but never completed, owing to his assassination in 743 CE. It is best known for its carved stone frieze on both sides of the entrance gate. A large part of the frieze (33 x 5 m / 108 x 16 ft) is now in the Pergamon Museum in Berlin, a gift from the Ottoman sultan Abdul Hamid II to the German emperor Wilhelm II in 1903. Its design structure features a horizontal zigzag, creating a pattern of triangular frames, inside which are delicately carved animals, flowers and leaves. Interestingly, the frames on the left of the entrance depict animals, while the frames on the right do not, possibly because the mosque was behind the right wall.

**UMAYYAD: QUSAYR 'AMRA, EASTERN DESERT, JORDAN** (723–743 CE)

This residential and agricultural complex in the middle of the Jordanian desert is famous for the frescoes in the bathhouse. The large triple-barrel-vaulted audience hall contains the fresco of the 'six kings': Roderic the Visigoth, the Byzantine emperor, the Sasanian emperor, the Ethiopian emperor and two other figures, thought to be a Turkic and a Chinese ruler. Other frescoes depict hunting scenes, musicians, bathing women, even a bear playing an instrument. The domed ceiling of the *calidarium* (a steamroom with underfloor heating) features the earliest known painting of the zodiac and the constellations of the northern hemisphere on a spherical surface. The imagery in all the frescoes is uniquely Umayyad; there are no precedents or parallels from the Byzantine or Sasanian eras.

## UMAYYAD: QASR KHARANA, EASTERN DESERT, JORDAN (710 CE)

Set in the middle of the Jordanian desert 60 km (40 miles) south of Amman, Qasr Kharana is one of the very earliest Umayyad monuments and part of a tradition of desert castles. It is a square structure, 35 m (115 ft) on each side (the approximate length of the 'actus', a Roman measurement), with towers on the corners and semicircular buttresses halfway along each wall. Its square courtyard has two levels of accommodation around it. It has some architectural features that the other desert castles in the area do not have: semi-domes and squinches, such as those seen in pre-Islamic Sasanian Iran. Some ornamental elements have been added by bricks placed at 45-degree angles and stucco ornamentation. The walls are mostly made of limestone blocks, and the narrow vertical openings in the wall serve to provide ventilation.

LEFT & BELOW

## AL-BIDYA MOSQUE, FUJAIRAH, UNITED ARAB EMIRATES (15TH C)

The second-oldest mosque in the UAE, it is located on the remote mountainous coastline in one of the UAE's constituent emirates, Fujairah. It is not known precisely when it was built, although a date of 1446 has been suggested. Made of mud and stone, covered in layers of plaster, the building is only 53 m² (570 sq ft) in area, with a single pillar in the middle. Four domes sit next to each other in a 2 x 2 arrangement. They are designed like increasingly smaller discs stacked on top of each other, with a small final protuberance on top. Each dome has a different number of discs, from one to four. The mosque's small plaster minbar (left) is worn from centuries of use.

OPPOSITE

## SHEIKH ZAYED GRAND MOSQUE, ABU DHABI, UNITED ARAB EMIRATES (2007)

The construction of the UAE's largest mosque was the initiative of the late president of the UAE, Sheikh Zayed bin Sultan Al Nahyan. It takes design inspiration from a range of historical mosques and eras and has capacity for 40,000 worshippers. Among its many opulent features, the stone inlay flower compositions on the mosque's faceted columns, made in India by Saray Design, stand out. They feature lapis lazuli, amethyst, onyx, agate, aventurine and mother-of-pearl, all inlaid in marble.

**FLYING SAUCER, SHARJAH,
UNITED ARAB EMIRATES** (1978)
The two sixteen-pointed stars that form
the roof make direct reference to the shape
and proportion of such stars in Islamic
geometric design. The building's central
dome is 7 m (23 ft) high and the roof is
supported by V-shaped pillars. Over the
years, it has been a café and a supermarket.
It has now been renovated and given an
underground extension to enable it to
function as a cultural venue. It was designed
by Egyptian architect Aly Nour El Din Nassar.
    The renovation of the Flying Saucer
was led by Sharjah Art Foundation and
SpaceContinuum Design Studio, helmed
by SpaceContinuum founder Mona El Mousfy.

## LOUVRE ABU DHABI, UNITED ARAB EMIRATES (2017)

Designed by architect Jean Nouvel, the museum is an arrangement of white flat-roofed structures, covered by an upturned shallow metal dish, surrounded by the turquoise waters of the Gulf. It is sited on Saadiyat Island, a developing cultural district for the capital of the UAE. The roof, weighing 7,500 tonnes, is made of eight layers of squares and equilateral triangles differing in scale and orientation, creating a dense mesh that diffuses sunlight into the space below, much as wooden *mashrabiyya* screens do.

**SALEM BIN LADEN MOSQUE,
AL-KHOBAR, SAUDI ARABIA** (1991)
This mosque is built on a small artificial
island along the Corniche of Al-Khobar.
It is dedicated to the memory of Salem
bin Laden, former chairman of the Saudi Bin
Laden Group, a huge company, responsible
for many of Saudi Arabia's main infrastructure
and construction projects. The mosque
applies familiar features and shapes, such as
dome, minaret and keel arches in a way that
synthesizes traditional with contemporary.

**KAFD GRAND MOSQUE, RIYADH, SAUDI ARABIA** (2017)

Built in the heart of King Abdullah Financial District, the mosque is surrounded by tall buildings, so its appearance from above is just as important as that from the more common viewpoints. Its low roof is composed of large, layered geometric shapes that transform into lozenge shapes to create the entrance façade. The architects, Omrania, took inspiration from the layered, crystalline structure of the desert rose – crystal clusters abundant in the deserts of Saudi Arabia. The interior is a single, uninterrupted space without columns thanks to a structural roof almost 3 m (10 ft) in depth, which also supports a floating mezzanine. Two angular 60 m (200 ft) minarets are placed on either side.

**AL-MASJID AL-HARAM, MECCA, SAUDI ARABIA** (EST. 7TH C CE)

Also known as the Great Mosque of Mecca, it surrounds the Kaaba, Islam's holiest place. The initial mosque structure on the site was built during the reign of Caliph Omar Ibn al-Khattab (634–644 CE), and over the centuries, it has been rebuilt, renovated and extended, so that it is now the largest mosque in the world, able to accommodate millions of pilgrims during the annual Hajj pilgrimage. It is the only mosque in the world without a qibla (indicating the direction of prayer towards the Kaaba).

## TULUNID: MOSQUE OF IBN TULUN, CAIRO, EGYPT (879 CE)

Ahmad ibn Tulun was the Abbasid governor in Egypt before he rebelled and established his own dynasty. He built a new capital in Egypt, but all that remains of what he built is his mosque, which greatly resembles the Abbasid architecture in Iraq (see p. 67). The arches around the central courtyard are elaborately decorated with a wide variety of patterns in carved plaster. The style of mosque would have been new to the local population, as was the fact that a drawing of the building (on animal skin) was presented to Ibn Tulun before construction commenced. In Egypt, buildings were constructed without drawings and the fact that it was different for this mosque was considered noteworthy. The ablutions fountain in the middle was built at the end of the 13th century by Mamluk sultan Lajin, who vowed to restore the mosque if he escaped with his life, after hiding there for a year following his complicity in the assassination of Mamluk sultan Qalawun.

## FATIMID: BAB AL-FUTUH, CAIRO, EGYPT (1087)

Bab al-Futuh is one of the gates for the recently founded Fatimid city of al-Qahirah (from where Cairo gets its name). All three gates were commissioned by the Fatimid vizier Badr al-Jamali, who used Armenian and Syrian masons. The combination of Fatimid decorative elements with the architectural (classical) legacy from northern Syria can be seen in all three towers. Above the entrance gate is a striking arched band made of diamond shapes filled with decorative elements. Two other city gates remain: Bab Zuwayla and Bab al-Nasr.

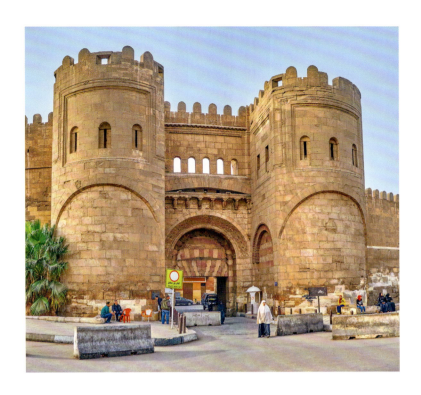

BELOW
**FATIMID: AL-AZHAR MOSQUE, CAIRO, EGYPT** (972 CE)
Originally built as the congregational mosque for the new city of al-Qahirah by Jawhar al-Siqilli, the Fatimid general who conquered Egypt, the mosque complex has been reworked, extended, reorganized and restored over more than a thousand years. Al-Azhar University was established in 988 CE, making it one of the oldest universities in the world. The keel arches around the courtyard are 12th-century Fatimid. During the Mamluk era, the complex was enlarged by the construction of adjacent madrasas. See also p. 32.

**FATIMID: AL-AQMAR MOSQUE,
CAIRO, EGYPT** (1125)

Over the centuries, as Cairo grew and its
urban fabric became more dense, almost all
buildings had to be designed to fit into an
existing street plan. This is the first example
in Cairo where the mosque's design has
been adapted to a street plan. The entrance
is not on an axis with the qibla wall (which is
oriented to Mecca), but instead the façade
with the entrance follows the street. It is also
the first mosque to have a decorated stone
façade. The keel arch decoration over the
central entrance that became so popular in
the architecture of Cairo is also seen here for
the first time.

**MAMLUK: MADRASA OF SULTAN
AL-NASIR MUHAMMAD IBN QALAWUN,
CAIRO, EGYPT** (1303)

Al-Nasir Muhammad's madrasa and
mausoleum are located right next to the
large hospital (*bimaristan*) and funerary
complex of his father, Sultan al-Mansur
Qalawun. Beneath the famous stucco
minaret is a Gothic entrance portal with a
pointed arch made from a single piece of
marble, taken by the brother of al-Nasir
Muhammad from a church in the city of
Acre, Palestine (now in Israel), the last
stronghold of the Crusaders. The first
storey of the minaret is four-sided and
covered in finely carved stucco, almost
like lace, possibly made by North African
craftsmen. The upper, octagonal part of
the minaret was added at a later date during
the Mamluk era. The madrasa was the first
in Cairo to have four iwans (vaulted portals
opening on to a courtyard), one for each
school of Sunni jurisprudence.

### ABOVE

### MAMLUK: SULTAN HASAN MOSQUE-MADRASA, CAIRO, EGYPT (1363)

Cairo's most expensive medieval mosque (above left in photograph) was funded by a combination of austerity measures, increased taxes and the wealth of emirs who died in the Black Plague. Its main façade is 145 m (475 ft) in length and 38 m (125 ft) tall in parts. The decoration of the enormous entrance is unfinished, but features two unusual fivefold star designs. When tessellated, these star designs create an idiosyncratic pattern that can also be seen in the Friday Mosque of Yazd, Iran (see p. 81), built around the same time. Four madrasas are located behind the corners of the courtyard, each dedicated to one of the four Sunni schools of jurisprudence. See also Doors of al-Mu'ayyad Sheikh Mosque on p. 32.

### RIGHT

### MAMLUK: AL-NASIR MUHAMMAD MOSQUE, CAIRO, EGYPT (1318)

The royal mosque of Cairo's Citadel, it is where the Mamluk sultans (and Ottoman pashas) performed their Friday prayers. Built for Sultan al-Nasir Muhammad by the architect al-Ibn al-Suyufi, the hypostyle mosque has a central courtyard with a dome over the mihrab area. The dome is supported by granite columns taken from ancient Egyptian temples. One of the mosque's minarets is especially unusual: it has two courses of zigzag bands, one vertical and the other horizontal. Its top is shaped like a garlic bulb and is entirely covered in green, blue and white tiles, a probable Mongol influence. In the background of the photograph, the Ottoman Muhammad Ali Mosque on the citadel is visible.

RIGHT
## MAMLUK: FUNERARY COMPLEX OF SULTAN QAYTBAY, CAIRO, EGYPT (1474)

It is located in the Northern Cemetery of Cairo, where many of the most magnificent late Mamluk monuments can be found. Sultan Qaytbay was one of the most active Mamluk patrons; eighty-five buildings were commissioned or restored by him, in Cairo, Alexandria, Syria, Palestine and Mecca. He inspected every building he commissioned and also encouraged his emirs to build. His buildings are renowned for their excellent architectural detailing and ornamentation, especially in stone carving. The dome of his funerary complex is without doubt the zenith of Mamluk stone carving. The stones for the dome were carved off-site and assembled to create a seamless design.

LEFT
## MAMLUK: MINARETS OF AL-AZHAR MOSQUE, CAIRO, EGYPT

LEFT TO RIGHT: MINARET OF QAYTBAY (1468), MINARET OF AQBAGHAWIYYA MADRASA (1340), MINARET OF QANSAH AL-GHURI (1510)

Architecture was a competitive political arena in Mamluk Egypt. Sultan Qaytbay's minaret is considered to be the most beautiful in Cairo. Qaytbay's successor, Sultan al-Ghuri, wanted to make an even more impressive minaret and his architects built the unusual double-finial structure. The Mamluks also built two new madrasas next to the mosque; the minaret of Aqbaghawiyya madrasa was remodelled during the Ottoman period by Emir Katkhuda, head of the Janissaries (elite infantry units) and responsible for a great deal of building and renovation in mid-18th-century Cairo (see also p. 35).

OPPOSITE
## MAMLUK: DOORS OF SULTAN AL-MU'AYYAD SHEIKH MOSQUE, CAIRO, EGYPT (1421)

The doors were originally made for the Sultan Hasan Mosque-Madrasa (see p. 31). When the Sultan died before completion, the doors were bought for the very small sum of 500 dinars by al-Mu'ayyad Sheikh for his own religious-educational complex (which he built on the site of a prison in which he was once held captive). The massive wooden doors are covered in bronze geometric compositions, featuring twelve- and sixteen-pointed star patterns, that are cleverly joined together.

RIGHT

**OTTOMAN: SABIL-KUTTAB OF KATKHUDA, CAIRO, EGYPT** (1744)

Cairo has many *sabil-kuttab*s, mostly built during the Mamluk era – public buildings, usually with two storeys, that comprise a *sabil* (fresh water dispensary) on the ground floor, and a *kuttab* (Quran school for children) on the first floor. Katkhuda was a senior officer of Mamluk heritage in the Ottoman era who built and restored over thirty buildings in Cairo. To replenish his *kuttab*, water carriers brought water from the river on donkeys and camels and poured it into an underground cistern so that passers-by could quench their thirst.

OPPOSITE

**BASUNA MOSQUE, BASUNA, EGYPT** (2019)

The village of Basuna in Upper Egypt has had a mosque for over 300 years, but it has had to be completely rebuilt twice. The 2019 Basuna Mosque, designed by architect Waleed Arafa, sits on the original site in the middle of the village, squeezed among the buildings and the graveyard. The single-shell dome is made from lightweight bricks; the staggered pattern is visible both inside and outside, with the roof system serving as windcatcher and skylight. The mosque also features an innovative cuboid muqarnas structure, illuminated and inscribed with square Kufic calligraphy on the cube faces.

OVERLEAF

**MAMLUK: AMIR KHAYRBAK MAUSOLEUM, CAIRO, EGYPT** (1502–1520)

Although built shortly after the Ottomans had conquered Egypt, in appearance this is still very much a Mamluk building. Emir Khayrbak was the Mamluk governor of Aleppo but changed sides to the Ottomans at the decisive battle of Marj Dabiq in 1516. The Ottoman sultan appointed him governor of Egypt. He had already built his mausoleum in Cairo in 1502 when he was still working for the Mamluks. Under the new Ottoman regime, he added a madrasa-mosque and *sabil-kuttab* to his mausoleum. He also annexed an adjacent early Mamluk palace as his residence. The complex has a high dome, elaborately carved with floral and other curvilinear designs.

ABOVE

**AYYUBID: GATE OF THE SERPENTS, CITADEL, ALEPPO, SYRIA** (12TH–13TH C)

This gate is named after its two knotted double-headed serpents or dragons. To reach the gate, attackers would have to pass through a first gate and go up the large steps on the bridge, while being shot at with arrows. Upon reaching the entrance block, they would turn right to the Gate of the Serpents and attempt to break down the large iron door while standing under machicolations (openings) from which hot oil was poured.

RIGHT

**AYYUBID: CITADEL, ALEPPO, SYRIA** (12TH–13TH C)

The Citadel of Aleppo is one of the most impregnable in world history, thanks in part to its location and in part to its enormous entrance block. The Citadel's current appearance is due mostly to Sultan al-Ghazi, son of Saladin, the founder of the Ayyubid dynasty. Al-Ghazi dug out a moat, built the imposing entrance block and covered the slopes of the Citadel in smooth limestone. These major projects were undertaken at a time when Aleppo was frequently under threat from Frankish (Crusader) forces. Despite the fortifications, the Mongols managed to capture the Citadel in 1260.

## UMAYYAD: UMAYYAD MOSQUE, DAMASCUS, SYRIA (C. 715 CE)

During the reign of the first Umayyad caliph, Muslims and Christians shared the use of the Cathedral of St John, the church that occupied the site of what would become the Umayyad Mosque. The sixth caliph, al-Walid I, took over the church site and built a new mosque, which became a model for all hypostyle mosques built in newly conquered territories. A large courtyard (*sahn*) was surrounded on three sides by arcades (*riwaq*s), with a covered prayer area (*haram*) on the fourth side.

**GREAT SELJUK: GREAT MOSQUE OF
ALEPPO MINARET, SYRIA** (1094)

The mosque itself is from the Umayyad era
but the minaret is later; it was commissioned
by a local judge (*qadi*) in the late 11th century.
Made of limestone, it is 45 m (148 ft) tall. It
is divided into five horizontal levels, with
detailing and decoration becoming more
refined and elaborate the higher up it goes.
Similarly with the calligraphy: the highest
level has a dedication in the name of God to
the Seljuk sultan; a level lower a dedication
to the Seljuk prince who ruled Aleppo;
below that the founder's name, *qadi*

Muhammad ibn al-Khashshab; below that a
text from the Quran blessing anyone who
builds a mosque; and at the lowest level, the
name of the architect, Hasan bin Mufarraj
al-Sarmani, and the date of construction.
The blind three-lobed (trefoil) arches that
wrap around the upper level are thought to
be the first occurrence of this arch design,
which later became popular in European
architecture. Considered to have been
the most beautiful minaret in Syria, it was
destroyed in 2013.

OPPOSITE

## ZENGID: BIMARISTAN NUR AL-DIN, DAMASCUS, SYRIA (1154)

This hospital and medical school is one of Damascus's most famous buildings. Its most striking feature is its muqarnas dome that rises high above the main entrance. Unusually, the outside of the dome shows what the inside looks like – there are only a handful of similar examples in Islamic architecture, most of them in Iraq. The dome is also pierced with small apertures, covered in coloured glass, allowing coloured light to filter into the building. It functioned as a hospital for over 700 years. The Mamluk sultan Qalawun was treated here and was so grateful for his recovery that he built a huge *bimaristan* (hospital) in Cairo, which became the model for most *bimaristan*s thereafter.

BELOW

## ZENGID: NUR AL-DIN MOSQUE, HAMA, SYRIA (1135)

The mosque is situated on the west bank of the Orontes River. In medieval northern Syria it was easy to find existing building materials: there were many ancient, classical and Christian ruins whose spolia could be repurposed. Sometimes elements from ruins were used conspicuously, either to make a positive connection to the past or, as is the case when Crusader spolia were used, to emphasize the demise of a reign. On either side of the mihrab in the mosque are two upside-down columns and capitals (possibly taken from the Crusader capital of Acre in Palestine, now in Israel). Hama is famed for its enormous waterwheels, or *noria*s. For centuries they have irrigated crops and provided water to the city. They make a distinctive sound as they turn, a bit like whale song, and can be heard at night across the city.

LEFT

## OTTOMAN: AS'AD PASHA KHAN, DAMASCUS, SYRIA (1753)

Constructed by the Ottoman governor of Damascus, As'ad Pasha al-Azem, the building was a caravanserai, or *khan*, serving as a centre of commerce, a guesthouse and a storage facility for merchants visiting the city. It has eighty rooms for lodgers. The enormous courtyard has eight domes plus a central open aperture. Underneath each dome are twenty arched windows that bring light into the courtyard. It is entirely made in the traditional 'ablaq' style of alternating rows of black and white stone.

**MOUNT LEBANON EMIRATE:**
**BEITEDDINE PALACE, LEBANON** (1818)

Lebanon was the most autonomous province
of the Ottoman Empire. Its architectural
traditions are remarkably consistent over
many centuries. The Ottoman practice
of employing local masons as masters of
construction prevailed, with masons building
in the style they were accustomed to.
Beiteddine Palace was built between 1788
and 1818 by Emir Bashir Shihab II. It has three
main courtyards, enormous vaulted stables,
guest apartments, water fountains and
domed hammams (Turkish baths). Its opulent
decoration has earned it the local nickname
of Lebanon's Alhambra.

LEFT

## UMAYYAD: KHIRBAT AL-MAFJAR, JERICHO, WEST BANK (743 CE)

A fortified desert palace near the Palestinian city of Jericho, Khirbat al-Mafjar (also known as Hisham's Palace) includes a mosque, a bathhouse, a palace and an audience hall. Its elaborate decoration in different materials (stucco and mosaic especially) gives a good idea of the tastes of the Umayyad caliphs. One large painted stucco sculpture shows a white-robed man with a beard and a sword, standing on the backs of lions. A famous mosaic depicts a leafy tree bearing fruit under which are three gazelles, one of which is being attacked by a lion. The very large mosaic floor of the bathhouse has more than thirty abstract designs, resembling a floor covered with rugs. The art and decoration show the influence of the cultures that preceded the Umayyads: Byzantine and Sasanian. The stucco panel with the human busts seen here was originally located in the palace entrance; its style is indebted to Sasanian art.

RIGHT

## UMAYYAD: WOODEN PANEL, AL-AQSA MOSQUE, JERUSALEM (8TH C CE)

Carved in a low-relief technique in cedarwood imported from Lebanon, this panel is one of several in al-Aqsa Mosque (see opposite and overleaf), all of exquisite quality. Their floral, vegetal and geometric designs are carved with great skill and intricacy, showing the excellence of woodcarving in the Umayyad period. They give a good insight into the taste of very early Islamic art in 8th-century Jerusalem and display influences from Sasanian, Coptic, Byzantine and local Syrian visual traditions.

ABOVE & LEFT

### UMAYYAD: WELL OF SOULS AND MIHRAB OF SULEIMAN, JERUSALEM (C. 7TH–8TH C CE)

The Dome of the Rock (see p. 12) was built above an exposed bedrock, known as the Noble Rock (or to Jews as the Foundation Stone). The rock, from which Muhammad is believed to have ascended to Heaven, has a hole in it, providing light and air to a small cave below. The cave is said to have been created when the Noble Rock wanted to follow Muhammad to Heaven. As the archangel Gabriel restrained the stone, he left his handprint. The cave, known as the Bi'r al-Arwah (Well of Souls) has great significance to all three Abrahamic faiths. It houses the Mihrab of Suleiman (left), considered to be Islam's earliest mihrab.

OVERLEAF

### UMAYYAD: AL-AQSA MOSQUE, JERUSALEM (EST. 690 CE)

The mosque is located on the holy site known by Muslims as the Haram al-Sharif (Noble Sanctuary) and by Jews and Christians as the Temple Mount. Built by Umayyad caliph Abd al-Malik, who also built the nearby Dome of the Rock (see p. 12), the mosque was enlarged by his son, al-Walid. Earthquakes in the 8th century CE necessitated its rebuilding by Abbasid caliphs. It owes most of its present appearance, including its façade, to a Fatimid rebuilding project after an earthquake in 1033.

The Crusaders who captured Jerusalem in 1099 mistakenly thought al-Aqsa Mosque was Solomon's Palace and the Dome of the Rock Solomon's Temple. In 1484, a German cleric, Bernhard von Breydenbach, published *Peregrinatio in Terram Sanctam*, documenting his travels in the Middle East. It became a 15th-century European bestseller and had a pervasive influence on the perception in Europe of the Middle East and Islam. In a large panoramic drawing of Ottoman Jerusalem, the Dome of the Rock, for example, is mislabelled as Solomon's Temple.

OPPOSITE

**MUSEUM OF ISLAMIC ART, DOHA, QATAR** (2008)

Built on an artificial peninsula in Doha Bay, the museum was designed by I. M. Pei, who at the age of nearly ninety was famously persuaded out of retirement to create it. Pei wanted the museum to be seen as a sculpture in itself. Constructed as stacked squares and octagons, its simple, strong shapes seek to embody the essence of Islamic architecture. Pei said he took his inspiration for the exterior form from the ablutions fountain in the centre of the Mosque of Ibn Tulun in Cairo (see p. 28), which he described as a severe architecture that comes alive in the sun, with its shadows and shades of colour.

ABOVE

**COLLEGE OF ISLAMIC STUDIES, HAMAD BIN KHALIFA UNIVERSITY, EDUCATION CITY, DOHA, QATAR** (2013)

This was constructed as one large building with many different functions, including a mosque, a library, faculty space and classrooms. The building's philosophy is based on a *külliye*, a traditional architectural complex that includes many different buildings (such as mosque, madrasa, soup kitchen). The connectedness of all educational facilities under one roof serves to encourage interaction between all users of the building and to create an environment where knowledge and faith are not separate. The mosque part is elevated above the ground, supported by five pillars (representing the Five Pillars of Islam). The building was designed by Mangera Yvars Architects.

OVERLEAF

**BEIT AL QURAN MUSEUM, MANAMA, BAHRAIN** (1990)

The Beit al Quran (House of Quran) is a multipurpose complex that includes a museum as well as a mosque, a madrasa and other spaces; the museum houses an important collection of Islamic art and Qurans. The prayer hall of the mosque is covered by a 16 m (52 ft) diameter stained-glass composition, featuring geometric patterns and calligraphy (Verse 18 of Surah al-Tawbah) by Egyptian master calligrapher Ahmad Mustafa. The window was designed and made by British stained-glass artist John Lawson.

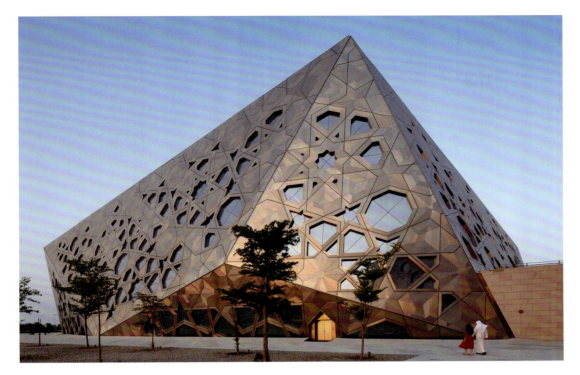

LEFT

**SHEIKH JABER AL-AHMAD CULTURAL CENTRE, KUWAIT CITY, KUWAIT** (2016)

Part of Kuwait's National Cultural District, the centre is also sometimes called the Kuwait Opera House. Its four buildings are arranged in a large landscaped area, creating small and medium-sized open spaces between them. Each building is covered in a metal and glass skin featuring a large-scale fourfold Islamic geometric pattern. The centre includes concert halls, theatres, libraries, a music centre, and conference and exhibition facilities. The entire complex was designed and built in only twenty-two months by SSH.

OPPOSITE

**AL-SHAWADNA MOSQUE, NIZWA, OMAN** (1529)

One of the oldest mosques of Oman, located in the Al Aqr district of the city of Nizwa, it was reportedly first built in the 7th century CE and then rebuilt in 1529, as an inscription on the mihrab indicates, during the reign of the Nabhani dynasty. Typical for traditional mosques in Oman, it is simple, and without adornment on the outside, and does not have a dome or minaret. The exceptional plaster mihrab, delicately decorated with floral and geometric motifs, was made by Issa bin Abdullah bin Youssef. Above the niche of the mihrab is a blue-and-white Chinese bowl, inserted in the plaster. In Kufic calligraphy at the top is the Shahada, the profession of faith and one of the Five Pillars of Islam.

ABOVE

**SULTAN QABOOS GRAND MOSQUE, MUSCAT, OMAN** (2001)

Inaugurated in 2001 by the Sultan of Oman to celebrate thirty years of his reign, the mosque was designed by Iraqi architect Mohamed Makiya. It has five minarets, one taller than the others, representing the Five Pillars of Islam. The ornamentation of the mosque explicitly uses styles and contributions from around the world, emphasizing an inclusive and universal vision. An exterior arcade with niches features a range of ceramic and glass mosaics, such as the one seen here. The calligraphy is by Sheikh Hilal al Rahawy, Oman's most respected calligrapher. The design of the niche composition is by Edman O'Aivazian.

**TAHIRID: AL-AMIRIYA MADRASA, RADA, YEMEN** (1504)

Commissioned by the last Tahirid sultan, the madrasa was built not far from the Rada citadel (seen in the background of the photograph). Measuring 40 x 23 m (131 x 75 ft), it has a row of shops on the outside and a hammam (public bath) at the southwest corner. The prayer hall is on the first floor and is elaborately decorated in stucco and painted geometric and floral patterns. The madrasa was restored over two decades by Iraqi archaeologist Selma al-Radi, for which she was given the 2007 Aga Khan Award for Architecture. Her project enabled local workers to learn traditional building skills, such as the use of *qudad*, a waterproof mortar used on the exterior. Made of lime and volcanic aggregate, it is polished with a smooth stone and daubed with animal fat.

**RASULID: MOSQUE AND MADRASA OF AL-ASHRAFIYYA, TAIZ, YEMEN** (1297)

Paint and stucco were the two dominant forms of decoration in Rasulid architecture. Most Rasulid buildings have been lost to time, but descriptions indicate that only the sultans had their buildings painted on the inside – everyone else had to use plain stucco. The Mosque and Madrasa of al-Ashrafiyya has both stucco and painted decoration in abundance. They offer a combination of calligraphy, geometric (rectilinear) patterns and floral (curvilinear) designs, balancing each other. The white stucco surfaces juxtaposed with the painted surfaces also provide a balance.

OPPOSITE

**SULAYHID: QUEEN ARWA MOSQUE, JIBLA, YEMEN** (1111)

Initially built as a palace, it was transformed into a mosque when Queen Arwa (see p. 314) moved the Sulayhid capital from Sana'a to Jibla. Pointed arches of different sizes surround the courtyard. Arwa's tomb is located in a corner of the mosque. Carved stucco has been used to decorate surfaces.

ABOVE

**QABR NABI HUD, WADI HADRAMAUT, YEMEN** (DATE UNKNOWN)

Four days a year, pilgrims come to worship the Prophet Hud, who lived in pre-Islamic times and has a chapter in the Quran named after him. The houses of the deserted village around his tomb (*qabr*) fill up with pilgrims for this brief period. Inside the prayer hall of Qabr Nabi Hud is the rock on which Hud is said to have stood when he called on the wealthy people of Aad to worship God and renounce their idols.

# 2

# Iraq, Iran & South Asia

Baghdad was founded in 762 CE as the capital of the Abbasid Caliphate. Built from scratch, it must have been an extraordinary place to visit. A 10th-century historian, Yakut al-Hamawi, describes the city:

> *The city of Baghdad formed two vast semi-circles on the right and left banks of the Tigris, twelve miles in diameter. The numerous suburbs, covered with parks, gardens, villas, and beautiful promenades, and plentifully supplied with rich bazaars, and finely built mosques and baths, stretched for a considerable distance on both sides of the river. In the days of its prosperity the population of Baghdad and its suburbs amounted to over two [million]! The palace of the Caliph stood in the midst of a vast park several hours in circumference, which beside a menagerie and aviary comprised an enclosure for wild animals reserved for the chase. The palace grounds were laid out with gardens and adorned with exquisite taste with plants, flowers, and trees, reservoirs and fountains, surrounded by sculpted figures. On this side of the river stood the palaces of the great nobles. Immense streets, none less than forty cubits wide, traversed the city from one end to the other, dividing it into blocks or quarters, each under the control of an overseer or supervisor, who looked after the cleanliness, sanitation and the comfort of the inhabitants.*

The scale and originality of their architecture – enormous palaces, minarets and mosques – shows the Abbasids' confidence and ambition. At 239 x 156 m (784 x 512 ft) and surrounded by a very

**ZAND: VAKIL MOSQUE, SHIRAZ, IRAN** (1773)

The mosque was built for Karim Khan, ruler of the Zand dynasty, in his capital city. He is revered as possibly Iran's most benign ruler. Such was his kindness that it is said he invited musicians to play music during construction of the mosque for the benefit of the builders. The building has two iwans instead of the usual four. Its *shabestan* (night prayer hall, see photograph) has forty-eight carved spiral columns. Much of the magnificent tilework was done in the 19th century during the Qajar era.

OPPOSITE

**SAFAVID: TOMB OF SHEIKH SAFI AL-DIN, ARDABIL, IRAN** (16TH C)

Sheikh Safi al-Din was the founder of the Safawiyya Sufi order, which gave rise to the Safavid empire. The shrine complex, with its mosque, mausolea, prayer hall, school, public baths, kitchens, offices and other spaces, resembles a small city, and has been a place of pilgrimage for centuries. Sheikh Safi al-Din's tomb itself is a domed, cylindrical tower decorated with exquisite mosaic tilework. The famous Ardabil carpet (one of the largest and most beautiful carpets in the world, now in the Victoria and Albert Museum in London) was made for the shrine of Sheikh Safi al-Din.

large walled enclosure (*ziyada*), the 9th-century Great Mosque of Samarra (see p. 67) was the largest in the world. The Abbasids had a great impact on the decorative styles and architectural features that pervade Islamic architecture; their two- and three-dimensional geometric compositions were complex and sophisticated, their distinctive bevelled Samarra stucco (see p. 66) timeless and innovative. Abbasid architecture, in its detail, buildings and city planning, shows us their desire to innovate. Their attitude to architectural and design knowledge – how to acquire it and how to apply it – was part of the ethos of the Golden Age of Islam, the term used to describe Abbasid Baghdad from the 8th to the 13th century. (It came to an end when the Mongols sacked the city in 1258.) The Mongols later founded their own city, Soltaniyeh, capital of their short-lived Ilkhanid empire, or Ilkhanate. All that remains of this city is an enormous tomb complex (see p. 78), which contains the world's third-largest brick dome. This is the tomb of Ilkhanid ruler Uljaytu, who, perhaps indicative of the time and place in which he lived, was baptized as a Nestorian Christian and raised as a Buddhist, and then converted to Islam. The tomb complex is one of the masterpieces of Islamic architecture, in both its structure and its geometric compositions. Many exceptional buildings in Soltaniyeh (and other cities, such as Tabriz) were demolished by a son of the Turkic conqueror Timur (1336–1405).

Some of the most significant monuments of Islamic architecture were built in the 10th to 13th centuries in Iran. New forms were developed, such as the four-iwan mosque, as can be seen in the Friday Mosque of Isfahan (see p. 73). The strikingly sharp geometric shape of the 11th-century Gonbad-e Qabus, an immensely tall brick mausoleum (see p. 72), also speaks of confidence and ambition. Most of all, the architecture of Iran is a combination of strength, imagination and refinement. This is exemplified in the Shrine of Pir-i Bakran (see p. 79), with its beautifully carved stucco mihrab, and calligraphic compositions on the arched ceiling and walls created with glazed and unglazed bricks. Iran also gives us geometric compositions made with small pieces of mirror glass (*aina-kari*), as seen in the famous Shah Cheragh Shrine Complex in Shiraz (see p. 78). The Ali Qapu Palace in Isfahan has its music room with dozens of carved niches in the shape of vases, cups and jars (see p. 85). Such a room, or *chini-khana* (a building for precious Chinese porcelain), was first seen under the Timurids, used by the Safavids in Isfahan and then became part of the Mughal architectural

ABOVE

**GREAT SELJUK: STUCCO PANEL, IRAN**
(12TH C)

Excavated from a site in or near the city
of Rayy in Iran, the monumental panel,
measuring 151 x 343 cm (59 x 135 in), is made of
carved plaster. It has an underlying structure
of interlaced eight-pointed stars and cross
shapes. Clockwise from top left: a standing
figure holding a mace; four seated figures
drinking and listening to a tambourine
player; a prince on a throne, with attendants;
two seated figures and harp, violin and
tambourine players; a single standing figure;
the *hajib* (court official) chasing a man with
his stick, and a kneeling woman; the *hajib*
(with stick) and attendants; two figures
standing around a cypress tree flanked by
attendants; the *hajib* with the mace bearer,
the napkin bearer (master of robes) and one
bearing a hare, and other attendants; three
figures prostrating in front of the *hajib*.

OPPOSITE

**DELHI SULTANATE: QUTB MINAR, DELHI,
INDIA** (BEGUN C. 1198, COMPLETED 1369)
Built of red sandstone and marble, this
is India's tallest monument and one of
the world's tallest stone towers. With a
diameter of just over 14 m (46 ft) at its base,
the tower tapers off to 3 m (10 ft) at its full
height of 72.5 m (238 ft). The minaret and its
mosque, built in the middle of a Hindu fort,
commemorate the Islamic conquest of Delhi
in 1193 by Muhammad of Ghur, in modern-
day western Afghanistan. It is likely it was
inspired by the Ghurid Minaret of Jam, built
approximately a decade earlier (see p. 152).

design, where just the outlines of the vases, cups and jars remained
(see p. 100). Something that started as a way to display precious
objects evolved over the centuries and across the region to become
a visual decorative element signifying opulence and value.

Mughal architecture is designed to engage with us from a
distance (see the Taj Mahal complex, p. 94) but also to delight us
up close. The detail of craftsmanship, the delicate touch in, for
example, the depiction of flowers and leaves in stone inlay – they
all speak to Mughal sophistication. One of the most surprising finds
for this book was the stone ceiling of the Mughal-era Mosque of
Champaner in Gujarat (see p. 93). The design is like a fractal, created
by masons who also worked for clients of other faiths. The Mughal
Empire was founded by Babur (r. 1526–1530), a descendant of Timur.
This connection can be seen, especially, in the monumentality of
Mughal architecture. But India is more than Mughal architecture
and Mughal architecture is more than India. On the subcontinent,
there are the beautifully painted wooden mosques in Baltistan (see
p. 96), the unique mihrab of the 16th-century mosque of Bijapur
(see p. 93), the amazingly detailed and delicate carved terracotta of
the Adina Mosque in India (see p. 91)... the list goes on. Bangladesh
is the country with some of the most interesting and diverse modern
Islamic architecture, not just prize-winning mosques but also less
well-known examples, built and paid for by local communities.
Designs often defy categorization, such as the mosque with a sea of
small yellow domes near Tangail (see p. 107). Such mosques appear
across the world and give an insight into how the local faithful seek
to honour their Creator through architecture.

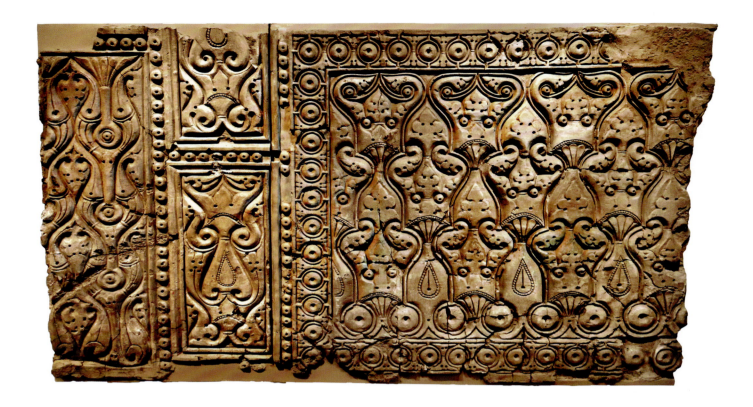

**ABBASID: STUCCO WALL PANEL FROM
A PRIVATE HOUSE, SAMARRA, IRAQ**
(9TH C CE)

The three styles of carving of the stucco
wall compositions of the Abbasid era are a
valuable tool for archaeologists to date sites,
showing as they do an evolution of early
Islamic imagery. Style A has carved leaves
surrounded by circular vines, indebted to
the Hellenistic style. Style B still has leaves
but no vines, and some straight lines. Both
A and B are made by carving and drilling
into the plaster. Style C, seen here, uses a
wooden mould, pressed into the wet plaster.
It is much more abstract, although in spirit
it still seems to represent natural forms. The
pattern was enhanced by polishing and the
occasional application of coloured pigment.

**ABBASID: GREAT MOSQUE OF SAMARRA,
IRAQ** (851 CE)

The ruins of the Abbasid capital of Samarra
in Iraq cover an area around 57 km² (22 sq
miles) along the banks of the Tigris River.
Caliph al-Mutawakkil was the greatest
builder of Samarra, credited with building
no fewer than nineteen palaces. The
Great Mosque – at the time of its building
the largest mosque in the world – has a
distinctive spiral minaret known as the
Malwiya Minaret. The Abu Dulaf Mosque
built by al-Mutawakkil a few years later
has a similar minaret; both mosques also
have a *ziyada*: a large walled area around
the mosque that contained, for example,
ablution fountains, medical facilities and
law courts. (Ibn Tulun mosque in Cairo was
very much influenced by Abbasid mosque
architecture and has a *ziyada*; see p. 28.)

### AL-SHAHEED MONUMENT, BAGHDAD, IRAQ (1983)

Designed by Iraqi artist Ismail Fatah Al Turk, the monument – also known as the Martyr's Memorial – is built on a circular platform 190 m (623 ft) in diameter, in the middle of an artificial lake. The dome, split into two halves, is covered in turquoise tiles – six slightly different shades of turquoise were used to give a more organic impression. Originally dedicated to those who died in the eight-year Iran–Iraq war, over the decades the monument has grown in meaning and relevance for all Iraqis, as sadly most will have friends and family members who have given their lives in war and conflict.

### ABBASID: TOMB OF SITT ZUMURRUD KHATOUN, BAGHDAD, IRAQ (1193)

Built by an Abbasid caliph for his mother, the mausoleum has a nine-layered muqarnas composition whose structure and shape can also be seen on the outside. Small holes create a delicate lighting effect in the interior. The muqarnas dome sits on an octagonal base decorated on the outside with *hazarbaf* brickwork (brickwork in relief to create a pattern) set into large square panels. There are very few muqarnas domes like this; there is an earlier one in Samarra, the tomb of Imam Dur, where the muqarnas elements are much larger, and the dome on the *bimaristan* of Nur al-Din in Damascus (see p. 43).

**BELOW**

**ABBASID: MIHRAB, ABBASID PALACE, BAGHDAD, IRAQ** (1175–1230)
The palace is a two-storey brick building on the bank of the Tigris River. Built during the late Abbasid era, it might possibly in fact have been a madrasa. Its central courtyard is surrounded with arches from behind which muqarnas compositions drape like curtains. The mihrab came from elsewhere, from near the city of Anah in Iraq.

**RIGHT**

**IMAM ALI MOSQUE, NAJAF, IRAQ** (EST. C. 786 CE)
Imam Ali was a cousin of the Prophet Muhammad and the first Shia imam. There are three tombs: one for Imam Ali and, according to Shi'ite belief, two for Adam and Nuh (Noah). Abbasid caliph Harun al-Rashid was the first to build a tomb over Imam Ali's tomb in 786 CE. Over the centuries, it has been extended, restored, rebuilt and embellished. As it is now, the complex's perimeter makes a square of roughly 120 m (394 ft) per side. In the middle sits the shrine building with its golden iwan, golden minarets and golden dome.

**IMAM ALI MOSQUE, NAJAF, IRAQ**
(EST. C. 786 CE)

**OTTOMAN: MAP OF NAJAF BY MATRAKÇI NASUH** (1534)

The left-hand page shows the city of Najaf, while the right-hand page depicts the Imam Ali Mosque (see previous page). It was drawn by the 16th-century Ottoman polymath Matrakçi Nasuh, who wrote at least four volumes of Ottoman history, illustrated with wonderfully detailed topographical views of various cities in the Ottoman Empire. Rivers, hills and buildings are recognizable.

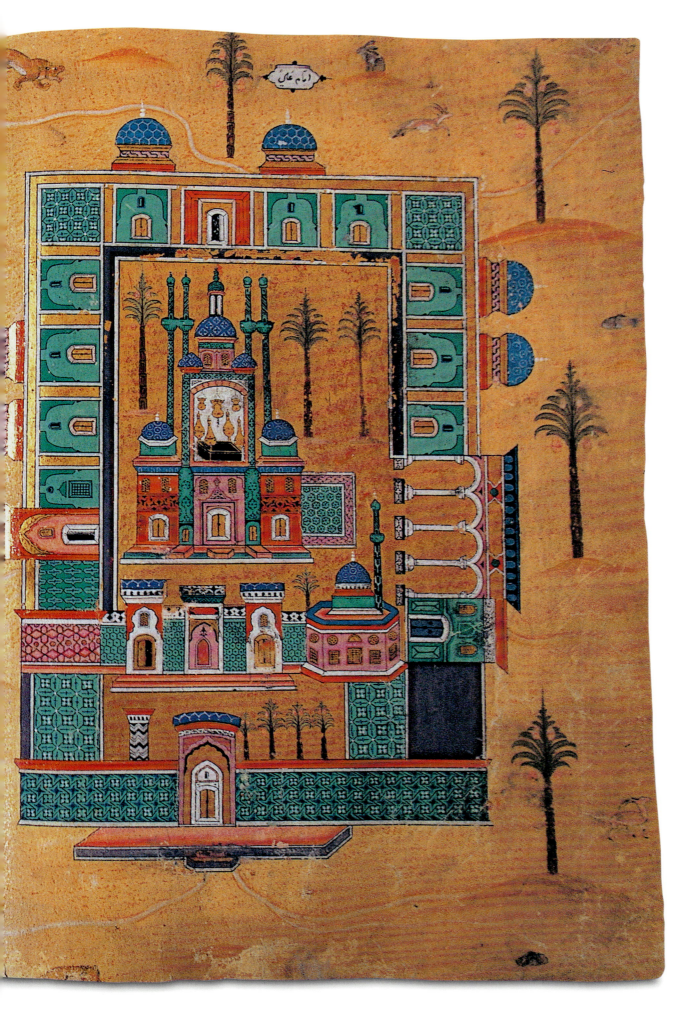

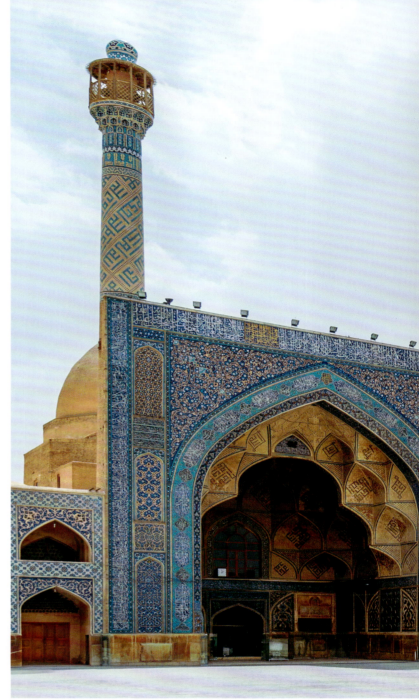

## ABOVE
## ZIYARID: GONBAD-E QABUS, GOLESTAN PROVINCE, IRAN (1007)

Built for the Ziyarid ruler Qabus, the tower is 53 m (174 ft) tall and almost 10 m (33 ft) in diameter at its base. It was built on an artificial hill and can be seen from a distance of 30 km (20 miles). It features some of the earliest muqarnas compositions in all of Islamic architecture, just above the main entrance. The tower is constructed of long, thin baked bricks. There is no evidence that Qabus was buried in his tower, but according to legend, his body was placed in a glass coffin suspended from the ceiling.

**OPPOSITE, BELOW**

**GREAT SELJUK: DOME CHAMBER OF TAJ AL-MULK, FRIDAY MOSQUE OF ISFAHAN, IRAN** (1089)

The purpose of this initially free-standing domed chamber, part of Isfahan's great Friday Mosque, has never been properly understood. It was built for Terkan Khatun (see p. 314), wife of the sultan, by the vizier Taj al-Mulk. Thirty-two of the ninety-nine names of God are written in the ring below the dome. Quranic verses are written in motifs formed by bricks on the inside of the dome. The dome chamber is considered one of the design milestones of Islamic architecture: Golden Ratio proportions inform all its aspects. There is some evidence to suggest that the designer was poet and polymath Omar Khayyam.

**ABOVE**

**GREAT SELJUK: FRIDAY MOSQUE OF ISFAHAN, IRAN** (EST. C. 771 CE)

The Great Seljuks made Isfahan their capital and between 1085 and 1125 transformed the existing hypostyle Friday mosque into a previously unseen four-iwan mosque: a large central courtyard (65 x 55 m / 213 x 180 ft) with arched entrances (iwans) on all four sides, and a large dome over the area in front of the mihrab. This became the standard mosque design in Iran and Central Asia. A smaller dome was built on the opposite, northern side of the mosque, considered to be a masterpiece of proportion, beauty and skill (see opposite). Over the centuries, many rulers and officials have made additions and alterations to the mosque.

**TARIKHANEH MOSQUE, DAMGHAN,
IRAN** (9TH C CE)

The oldest mosque in Iran, Tarikhaneh
('house of God') was built on the site of a
Zoroastrian fire temple. It was built using pre-
Islamic Sasanian construction techniques
and materials, as can be seen by the massive
round piers, almost 2 m (6 ft 6 in) in diameter.
The minaret in the background is from a later
period, built by the Great Seljuks in 1026–29.

**FRIDAY MOSQUE OF QAZVIN, IRAN**
(807 CE)

The mosque's construction was ordered by
Abbasid caliph Harun al-Rashid. It has one of
the largest courtyards of any Iranian mosque,
at over 4,000 m² (43,000 sq ft). Much of its
expansion occurred under the Great Seljuks
in the 12th century, when a courtyard, dome,
madrasa, main prayer hall and two iwans
were added. The prayer hall features some of
the most excellent Kufic calligraphy, carved
in plaster. Such is its quality that it is still used,
nine centuries later, for research and as a
benchmark of skill.

**GREAT SELJUK: RIBAT-I SHARAF
CARAVANSERAI, KHORASAN, IRAN**
(EARLY 12TH C)

This rest stop for travellers is located
in the desert on the road between Merv
(present-day Mary, Turkmenistan) and
Nishapur (Neyshabur, Iran) on the Silk
Road and part of a Shia pilgrim route. It
has two courtyards, one for royalty and
officials, and one for ordinary travellers.
It is famous for its elaborate decorative
brickwork. Built by the Seljuk governor
of Khorasan, it was heavily damaged by
nomads shortly after its construction.
It was restored in 1154 by Terkan bint
al-Kaghan, the wife of Sultan Sanjar.

**GREAT SELJUK: ALAVIAN DOME, HAMEDAN, IRAN** (c. 1315)
Originally built as a mosque with minarets and a dome, it later became the mausoleum for the Alavian family. Above the entrance is an extraordinarily exuberant three-dimensional plaster composition, added during the Ilkhanid era. Above this is a brick geometrical composition featuring tenfold star patterns, connected to each other with kite shapes. The interior decoration is similarly opulent, combining curvilinear, fluid shapes in plaster with the rectilinear, crystalline shapes of geometric design.

OPPOSITE

### ILKHANID: SHRINE OF PIR-I BAKRAN, NEAR ISFAHAN, IRAN (1303–12)

Sufi sheikh Pir-i Bakran lived, taught and died here. After his death in 1303, the Ilkhanids created a shrine complex, famous for its stucco and tile decorations, as well as its calligraphic panels. In 1309–10, the Ilkhanids changed their state religion from Sunni to Shia Islam, which had an impact on the calligraphic compositions. In the third phase of decoration (after 1310), two large square panels of Kufic script were added on opposite sides of the main iwan hall.

ABOVE

### INJUID: SHAH CHERAGH SHRINE COMPLEX, SHIRAZ, IRAN (1343)

Shiraz is known as the 'city of a thousand shrines' and this is the most important one. It houses the tombs of Ahmad and Muhammad, sons of the seventh imam in Twelver Shia Islam. They died in Shiraz in the 9th century. It features an exquisite and exceptionally pointed dome covered in floral ceramic tile patterns in turquoise, gold and white. The interior of the shrine is covered in millions of pieces of faceted mirror glass, an Iranian design tradition called *aina-kari*. The tomb was founded by Tashi Khatun, mother of the Injuid sultan.

RIGHT

### ILKHANID: TOMB OF ULJAYTU, SOLTENIYEH, IRAN (1313)

The city of Solteniyeh, founded around 1285, was made the capital of the Ilkhanid empire by Sultan Uljaytu in 1313. The walls of the citadel were described as being wide enough for four horsemen to ride abreast. The largest monument inside the citadel is the Tomb of Uljaytu. It is an enormous octagonal building, 38 m (135 ft) in diameter, with one of the largest brick domes in the world, surrounded by eight minarets.

OPPOSITE

**ILKHANID: FRIDAY MOSQUE OF YAZD, IRAN** (1324)

Built on the site of an earlier mosque, it has had much added to it over the centuries. Its most striking exterior features are the two tall minarets, rising from the top of the *pishtaq* (arched entrance). It is modelled on the now no longer extant Friday Mosque of Solteniyeh, as seen in a 1537 drawing by Matrakçi Nasuh. Its interior decorative scheme, mostly done during the reign of the Muzafarrids in the 14th century, is a superb and visually overwhelming array of blue and beige brick compositions (*hazarbaf*). The long vaulted ceilings feature square Kufic composition in *hazarbaf*, while the central dome is one of the masterpieces of Islamic dome interiors: blue and white bricks and tiles create a complex sixteen-fold geometric star composition. Compositions on dome interiors and exteriors are commonly multiples of four because of the convenient visual transition from the four sides of the structure it sits on.

ABOVE

**ILKHANID: KIRMANI MOSQUE, TURBAT-I SHAYKH JAM, KHORASAN, IRAN** (1363)

The mosque is named after Khwaja Masoud Kirmani, the artist who made the carved stucco mihrab seen here. He was later buried inside the mosque. Kirmani Mosque was part of a large complex of ten buildings built in honour of Sufi theologian and poet Sheikh Ahmad-i Jami. The shrine complex, built in phases, was the most visited pilgrimage site in Eastern Iran for several centuries. Two small mosques are sited on either side of the entrance portal, announcing a later trend for symmetry in architecture.

OVERLEAF

**MUZAFFARID: FRIDAY MOSQUE OF KERMAN, IRAN** (1350)

Kerman has been a major city for commerce for centuries. Marco Polo visited in the 13th century and claimed it had the best falcons in the world. Unusually, it has two Friday mosques, close both to each other and to the bazaar; the older was built by the Seljuks. The mosque built by the Muzaffarids in 1350 is considered one of the best examples of mosque architecture in Iran, particularly for its abundance of geometric, floral and vegetal tile decorations, as well as exquisitely made calligraphic bands in ceramic.

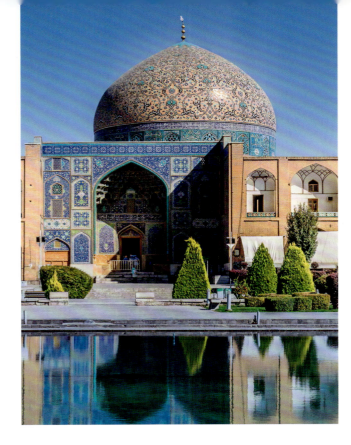

**SAFAVID: SHEIKH LOTFOLLAH MOSQUE, ISFAHAN, IRAN** (1617)
The mosque was built during the reign of Shah Abbas I as his personal mosque by architect Muhammad Reza Isfahani. Sheikh Lotfollah was the father-in-law of Shah Abbas I and a renowned imam. It is a huge square chamber without minarets and without a courtyard – more like a mausoleum than a mosque in style. The eight huge arches that support the drum upon which the dome sits are outlined in bright turquoise-blue ceramic twisted cables. The entire surface of the dome interior is covered with a network of leaf shapes, outlined in baked brick, diminishing in size as they go towards the apex of the dome and thus also creating a further impression of height.

### SAFAVID: MUSIC ROOM, ALI QAPU PALACE, ISFAHAN, IRAN (1597)

The top floor of the Ali Qapu Palace was used for banquets and official receptions, and is also the location of the music room. This room is designed as a *chini-khana*, a room for displaying precious Chinese porcelain. Such rooms first appeared in the Timurid era. The walls and ceilings of the music room are covered in niches in the shapes of vases, rosewater sprinklers, cups and jars. There are about 600 niches in total. The design of the music room may have been motivated by aesthetics, but the niches do give the room very good acoustic properties.

### SAFAVID: CHEHEL SOTOUN, ISFAHAN, IRAN (1647)

One of two remaining pavilions of a palace complex, Chehel Sotoun means 'forty columns' and refers to the twenty columns of the entrance porch, which when reflected in the pool in front seem to be forty. The interior surfaces are mostly covered in wall paintings. Besides the painted geometric and floral ornamentation, there are six large figurative paintings. These show either a Safavid shah receiving a ruler, or battle scenes, such as the one seen below – the 1514 Battle of Chaldiran against the Ottomans (which the Safavids lost!). On the verandas are panel paintings of different figures, including people in European dress.

RIGHT
### QAJAR: NASER EL MOLK MOSQUE, SHIRAZ, IRAN (1888)

A kaleidoscopic building, this mosque has an abundance of colour, light, pattern and texture. Its *orosi* (stained-glass) windows, made of coloured glass set in wooden grooved segments, illuminate the interior. Locals call it the Pink Mosque because of the use of this colour in tiles. It was commissioned by a son for his father (Naser el Molk), who had passed away in his absence. It also features some exceptionally complex muqarnas and *karbandi* (ornamental interlaced ribs) ceilings.

BELOW
### SAFAVID: SHAH MOSQUE, ISFAHAN, IRAN (1630)

Built on the maidan, the royal square of Isfahan, fifteen years after Shah Abbas I moved the capital of his empire to Isfahan, this mosque was the biggest project of Abbas's huge construction programme. The magnificent dome sits to the right of the entrance portal, in part so that it could be oriented towards Mecca and in part so that it was not obscured by the entrance. The winter prayer hall is shown below, its walls covered in tiles in the new *haft rangi* (seven colour) style of mosaic, in which tiles were painted with designs in many colours.

ABOVE
### QAJAR: TEKYEH DOWLAT, TEHRAN, IRAN (1868)

A royal theatre, especially famous for its performances of religious passion plays, Tekyeh Dowlat (State Theatre) was a large, three-storeyed rotunda with a circular platform with steps and ramps. On one side was a marble minbar from which a mullah directed the ceremonies. It had a vellum roof, draped over a domed wooden structure. According to many European visitors, its splendour and the dramatic intensity of its performances surpassed opera houses in European capitals. Construction started one year after that of the Royal Albert Hall in London, to which it bore a resemblance. It was demolished in 1946.

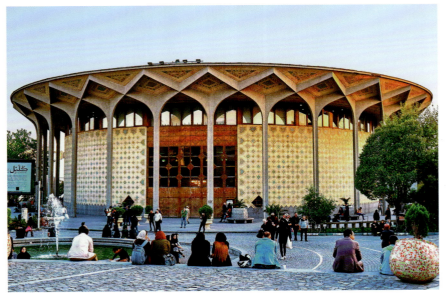

**TEHRAN CITY THEATRE, IRAN** (1972)
Designed by architect Ali Sardar Afkhami, the theatre has five performance spaces and is Iran's primary venue for theatrical productions. It measures 34 m (112 ft) in diameter and 15 m (49 ft) in height and is located in a corner of a city park. Its distinctive appearance is inspired by the Great Seljuk-era Tughril tomb tower in Rayy, Iran (1140). The theatre was built under the auspices of the empress Farah Pahlavi, and opened with a production of Chekhov's *Cherry Orchard*.

LEFT
**DELHI SULTANATE: QUTB MINAR, DELHI, INDIA** (BEGUN C. 1198, COMPLETED 1369)
Construction was started after the Ghurids from Afghanistan established themselves in India. It is similar to the minaret of Jam in Afghanistan (see p. 152) built only a decade or so earlier. See also p. 65.

OPPOSITE
**SHAH MIR: KHANQAH-E-MOULAH, SRINAGAR, INDIA** (1395)
Located on the right bank of the Jhelum River, it was built in honour of Syed Ali Hamdani, the 14th-century Muslim saint whose craftsmen built Amburiq Mosque (see p. 98). It is both a *khanqah* (a place of Sufi retreat) and a mosque. Its wooden architectural style is typical of the region and combines influences from Islamic, Hindu and Buddhist architecture. The call to prayer is performed by the muezzin from the square structure in the middle of the roof, known as the *mazina*. The spire in the middle represents the minaret.

RIGHT
**LODI DYNASTY: JAHAZ MAHAL, MANDU, INDIA** (2ND HALF 15TH C)
The Jahaz Mahal (Ship Palace) was built during the reign of Ghiyath Shah on a narrow strip of land between two artificial lakes. There were 12,000 women in his harem, including dancers, wrestlers and musicians, as well as 500 female bodyguards – young Turkish and Abyssinian women dressed in men's clothing. For all the women at the court, he built many baths, living quarters and pleasure domes. The Jahaz Mahal is one of those constructions. Water for the upper pool is brought up with a water lift and then passes through elaborately carved curvilinear channels, their shape serving to slow the momentum of the water so that it pours into the pool gently.

RIGHT

**BAHMANID: MAHMUD GAWAN
MADRASA, BIDAR, INDIA** (1472)

The madrasa is now mostly in ruins, but what remains indicates the magnificence of this important building. The madrasa offered free board, lodging and education to over 500 students and had a large library. The remaining ceramic tile compositions are framed in black basalt with glazed tile mosaic in dark blue, light blue, yellow, white and green. While the technique and skill were Iranian, the extra colours (yellow and green) indicate the use of pigments that were available in India but not in Iran. Added to this are underglaze tile mosaics in dark blue, light blue and white.

LEFT
**BENGAL SULTANATE: ADINA MOSQUE, PANDUA, INDIA** (1370)

Pandua became the capital of Bengal for a brief period in the second half of the 14th century. It was during this period that the Adina Mosque was built. For a time, it was the largest mosque on the Indian subcontinent, measuring 154 x 87 m (505 x 285 ft). Similar in plan to the Umayyad Mosque in Damascus (see pp. 11 and 40), it has a prayer hall with a 260-column hypostyle structure, a long, continuous façade towards the courtyard with ninety-two arches and a large rectangular courtyard. Basalt was used for the lower sections of many of the walls. Elaborately detailed brick and terracotta compositions feature in the mosque, often with unusual designs and themes borrowed from other cultures.

OPPOSITE
**LODI DYNASTY: BARA GUMBAD, LODI GARDENS, DELHI, INDIA** (1490)

This is considered to be the first dome building constructed in Delhi. 'Bara Gumbad' means 'big dome'. It is made of grey granite, grey quartzite, and red and cream-coloured sandstone. It is part of a group of three buildings, constructed at different times, built on a 4 m (13 ft)-high platform in what is now Delhi's Lodi Gardens. It is not clear what its original purpose was.

RIGHT
**GUJARAT SULTANATE: SIDI SAIYYED MOSQUE, AHMEDABAD, INDIA** (1572–73)

Renowned for its astonishing Gujarati sandstone *jali* (latticework) screens, the mosque was built just one year before Akbar brought the city under Mughal rule. Sidi Saiyyed was an Ethiopian ('Abyssinian') slave to the sultan, who later took a military role and built the mosque with the money he had acquired. At the time of construction, several thousand Abyssinians lived in Ahmedabad alone, they were traders and craftsmen or held powerful positions in government. Sidis are Indians of African Bantu descent; there are thought to be around 850,000 in India.

OPPOSITE
**ADIL SHAHI: FRIDAY MOSQUE OF BIJAPUR, INDIA** (1578)

One of the largest mosques of southern India, it is extensively decorated with murals around the mihrab, contrasting with its otherwise unadorned interior. Painted depictions include architectural structures, minarets, domes, arches, vases with flowers, niches with books and incense burners on chains, all in gold and blue. Directly above the mihrab niche are written 'Allah' and 'Muhammad', and there are numerous other calligraphic texts.

RIGHT
**MUGHAL: DIWAN-I KHAS, AGRA FORT, AGRA, INDIA** (1635)

This is a pavilion set inside the grounds of Agra Fort, where the Mughal emperor Shah Jahan could receive his courtiers and state guests. It has an inner hall, with a porch on all four sides. It is clad in marble, with many very fine stone inlay compositions of flowers. Its original ceiling was made in silver, with inlaid gold.

LEFT
**MUGHAL: FRIDAY MOSQUE OF CHAMPANER, INDIA** (1508)

The Friday Mosque of Champaner took twenty-five years to build and is considered to be one of the finest examples of Islamic architecture in western India. It shows the work of craftsmen and builders who also built for the Jain and Hindu communities. Above the central mihrab is this incredible, intricately carved stone composition, seemingly following the characteristics of fractal design. It is essentially the way a *kalpavriksha* is often depicted in regional architecture. A *kalpavriksha* ('world tree') is a wish-fulfilling holy tree in Hinduism, Buddhism and Jainism.

ABOVE

### MUGHAL: TAJ MAHAL, AGRA, INDIA (1632–1653)

This magnificent mausoleum was built by over 20,000 artisans for Emperor Shah Jahan to commemorate his favourite wife, Mumtaz Mahal, who died while giving birth to their fourteenth child. The white marble came from Rajasthan, and twenty-eight types of precious and semi-precious stones were used for inlay compositions. An enormous brick scaffolding was built for the construction of the dome, with a 16-km (10-mile) ramp leading to the site. Although there is no written architectural theory from the Mughal era, the Taj Mahal complex does demonstrate principles that were important in the architecture built during the reign of Shah Jahan: 1) geometrical planning, 2) symmetry, 3) hierarchy, 4) proportional formulas, 5) uniformity of shapes, 6) attention to detail, 7) use of naturalism, 8) symbolism. The entire complex was meant to evoke and represent the mansion of Mumtaz in the Garden of Paradise.

ABOVE

**MUGHAL: AKBAR'S TOMB, SIKANDRA, INDIA** (1613)

The tomb was built by the emperor Akbar's son, Jahangir. It is set in a square walled garden divided into four sections by watercourses, evoking the rivers of Paradise. This is the common *chahar bagh* ('four garden') design, seen in India and Iran. The tomb building is four storeys high, with sides of 105 m (345 ft). Each side has a tall *pishtaq* (arched entrance), with typically Indian *chhatri*s (roof kiosks).

RIGHT

**NAKHODA MOSQUE, KOLKATA, INDIA** (1926)

Kolkata's largest mosque was built by the Kutchi Memon Muslim community, who were mostly shipping merchants (*nakhoda* means a ship's captain) who moved to the city at the start of the 20th century. It was styled as an imitation of Akbar's tomb at Sikandra (see above right). The mosque has become the focal point around which Kolkata's Muslim culture developed and it is now the place where the first Eid prayers happen in the city. Built in red sandstone with emerald-green domes, it resembles a Mughal monument set right in the heart of a very busy shopping area.

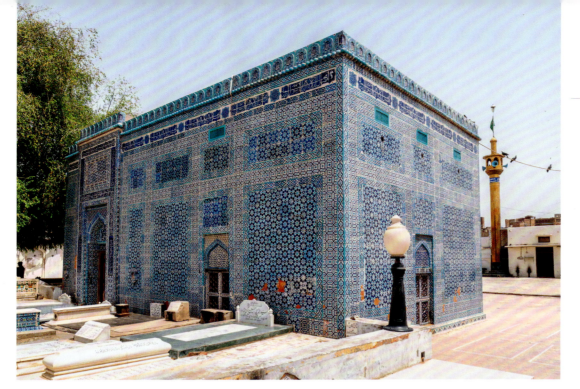

OPPOSITE

**CHAQCHAN MOSQUE, KHAPLU, PAKISTAN** (1370)

Set in the Khaplu Valley in Baltistan, the coldest place in Pakistan, it was built by Nurbakshia Sufis, and is one of the oldest mosques on the subcontinent. Constructed over two floors, it uses a structure of wooden beams with the voids filled with rubble and mud, making it better able to withstand earthquakes. Its wide wooden veranda, with a view of the Karakoram Mountains, has elaborate geometric wooden screens. Both men and women come to pray in its central space, which is constructed entirely of wood and beautifully painted on all surfaces. Four wooden columns occupy the centre of the space to support the roof.

ABOVE

**GHAZNAVID: MAUSOLEUM OF SHAH YUSUF GARDEZI, MULTAN, PAKISTAN** (1152)

Shah Yusuf Gardezi was the first Muslim saint on the Indian subcontinent. A simple rectangular building, his tomb is almost entirely clad in ceramic *kashikari* (hand-painted floral and geometric patterns) tiles.

There are apertures in the exterior for the many pigeons so that they can be close to the spot where the saint's body lies – according to legend, these are descendants of the pigeons that fluttered over the saint's head when he arrived in Multan on a lion in 1088, wielding a live snake as a whip. Near the door of the tomb lie the graves of the lion and the snake.

LEFT

**TUGHLUQID: TOMB OF SHAH RUKN-I ALAM, MULTAN, PAKISTAN** (1324)

The tomb was built by the founder of the Tughluq dynasty, Ghiyath al-Din, and later given to the descendants of the Sufi saint Shah Rukn-i Alam, after whom the tomb is now named. It is considered to be the finest example of a pre-Mughal Islamic tomb on the subcontinent. Octagonal in plan, it dominates the skyline of Multan. The tomb is much larger and more elaborate and refined in its decoration than other tombs in the area. Built of burnt brick, reinforced with rosewood timbers, the exterior is made of chiselled brick and glazed tiles in dark blue, azure and white, colours common in the ceramic traditions of Multan.

RIGHT

## AMBURIQ MOSQUE, SHIGAR, PAKISTAN (14TH C)

Islam first came to Baltistan in the 14th century through an Iranian Shia mystic, Syed Ali Hamdani, who brought with him craftsmen from Iran and Central Asia. They built Amburiq Mosque. Atop the tower on the roof is a wooden spire with four projecting beams called the *cholo*. From these beams would traditionally have hung wooden vase-like objects that often had thin 'wings'. Above the *cholo* is the *qubbah*, shaped like a small metal umbrella, from which chains hang. From these chains will hang a three-pronged *alam*, a commemorative metal object used in Shia Islam during the holiday of Ashura.

OPPOSITE

## MUGHAL: WAZIR KHAN MOSQUE, LAHORE, PAKISTAN (1641)

Wazir Khan was the royal physician to the court of Jahangir. He served at the court of Shah Jahan, son of Jahangir, became governor of Lahore and built many mosques, madrasas, caravanserais, palaces and baths in this city, as well as in his home town of Chiniot. His mosque has all the features that characterize his buildings: refined and extensive ornamental painting in warm, earthy tones, elaborate and bold tile mosaics (*kashikari*), frescoes outlined in brick, and stone and plaster decoration. Such is the diversity of its decoration that the mosque is like a design sourcebook that can be read. Unusually, it has a minaret on each corner.

ABOVE

## MUGHAL: NAULAKHA PAVILION, LAHORE FORT, PAKISTAN (1633)

'Naulakha' means 'nine lakhs' (900,000 rupees) in Urdu, an exorbitant amount of money to have been spent by Shah Jahan on this small pavilion in Lahore Fort. Clad in white marble from Makrana (India's oldest marble quarry, in Rajasthan), it is famous for its elegant curvilinear roof and for the quality and quantity of its *parchinkari* (inlaid precious and semi-precious stones).

The unusual roof shape (*jor-bangla*) is indebted to the indigenous architecture of Bengal. The large central *jali* (latticework) screen has a crown profile and an opening through which Shah Jahan could present himself to the public below. Seen from the ground, the *jali* screens of the pavilion sit atop Lahore Fort's famous 'picture wall', decorated with tiles, mosaics and frescoes.

**MUGHAL: TOMB OF JAHANGIR,
LAHORE, PAKISTAN** (1637)
The tomb took ten years to build and
occupies a very large quadrangle (500 x
500 m / 1,640 x 1,640 ft) divided into a grid
of squares that create four *chahar bagh*s
(gardens divided by two axes creating four
segments). The mausoleum sits at the
centre. It has four octagonal minarets on
the corners but, unusually, there is no dome
over the tomb. Large parts of the exterior are
decorated with designs of vases with flowers,
arches and bottles, made of white marble
inlaid in red sandstone. This design tradition
is called *chini-khana* (see p. 85). The interior
is elaborately and exquisitely embellished
with stone inlay compositions and richly
colourful frescoes on the walls and ceilings.

**SABRI MOSQUE, KARACHI,
PAKISTAN** (1945)
Sabri Mosque is one of the largest
mosques in Karachi, located in Ranchor
Line (Gazdarabad), one of the oldest
neighbourhoods of the city. Elaborately
decorated on almost all its surfaces with
white curvilinear floral and vegetal designs
on a dark red background, the mosque has
a full-size cricket ground in its back garden.

LEFT

**TALPUR DYNASTY: SHRINE OF SACHAL SARMAST, DARAZA SHARIF, SINDH, PAKISTAN** (19TH C)

Sachal Sarmast was a Sufi poet and a great lover of music. He spread his message of divine love through poems he wrote in seven languages (Sindhi, Siraiki, Persian, Urdu, Balochi, Punjabi and Arabic). He died at the age of ninety and a mausoleum was built by Talpur, ruler of Khairpur. It was later renovated and decorated with multicoloured glazed ceramics on the exterior and elaborate floral paintings on the inside.

BELOW

**MAZAR-E-QUAID, KARACHI, PAKISTAN** (1971)

Also known as the National Mausoleum or Jinnah Mausoleum, it was inaugurated twenty-three years after the death of Muhammad Ali Jinnah, founder of Pakistan. It was designed by Indian architect and friend of Jinnah, Yahya Merchant. Sited on a 75 x 75 m (246 x 246 ft) marble plinth, the mausoleum is clad in white marble and has a stucco dome, 43 m (141 ft) in height. It is approached via a terraced avenue with fifteen consecutive fountains in rectangular basins. It is modelled on the Tomb of the Samanids in Bukhara (see p. 139).

ABOVE

### BENGAL SULTANATE: SIXTY-DOME MOSQUE, BAGERHAT, BANGLADESH (MID-15TH C)

Built in a prominent location in the city of Khalifatabad, it is the largest historic mosque in Bangladesh. Its thick, tapering brick walls are more typical of pre-Mughal Delhi style. It actually has seventy-seven domes, seven of which are traditional Bengal *char-chala*-shaped vaults (made of four curved triangular sections that meet at the top and whose bottom corners curve downward). Khalifatabad flourished in the 15th century, with dozens of mosques and mausolea built in baked red brick. On the death of its founder, Khan Jahan Ali, the city was abandoned.

OPPOSITE

### PRAYER HALL, NATIONAL PARLIAMENT HOUSE, DHAKA, BANGLADESH (1983)

Construction on National Parliament House (Jatiyo Sangsa Bhaban) began when Bangladesh was still East Pakistan. Built over a period of more than twenty years, it was opened nine years after the death of its famous modernist architect, Louis Kahn. It is constructed of exposed concrete (an unconventional building material in Bangladesh); the horizontal bands are marble and were inserted after each day's concrete pour, at 1.5 m (5 ft) intervals. The prayer hall is on the entrance axis to the main building.

RIGHT

### SHAH MAHMUD MOSQUE, EGARASINDUR, KISHOREGANJ, BANGLADESH (1680)

The mosque stands on a raised platform with a gateway with a *do-chala* roof next to it (*do-chala* roofs are made of two curved rectangles joined at the top). It is a small square mosque, just under 6 m (20 ft) per side. It has octagonal towers at the corners and small arch designs on the exterior. Inside are three mihrabs, all elaborately embellished with carved terracotta designs.

**GULSHAN SOCIETY MOSQUE,
DHAKA, BANGLADESH** (2017)

A seven-storey mosque made of white cast concrete, it was designed by Kashef Chowdhury. The exterior pattern is made of abstracted letters that spell '*la ilaha illa Allah*' ('There is no God but Allah'). The available plot was not large enough to build a conventional mosque for the required number of worshippers, leading to this multistorey building. Bangladesh in the 21st century has become a leader in innovative and unconventional mosque design.

RIGHT

**RED MOSQUE, COLOMBO,
SRI LANKA** (1908)

Colombo, a port and Sri Lanka's largest city, has had a large Muslim population for centuries and was in need of a mosque big enough to accommodate the many faithful. Distinctive for its red and white stripes, the Red Mosque (also known as the Jami Ul-Alfar Masjid) was designed by an amateur architect, Habibu Labbe Saibu Labbe, who was helped with images of architecture shown to him by traders from South India. The original two-storey building features pomegranate-shaped domes. The mosque has been extended several times and can now accommodate 10,000 worshippers.

OVERLEAF

**201 DOME MOSQUE, SOUTH PATHALIA
VILLAGE, TANGAIL DISTRICT,
BANGLADESH** (2018)

The mosque's central dome rises 25 m (82 ft) and is surrounded by 200 smaller domes. The plan to build the mosque came from a local man, Rafiqul Islam, who realized that his village mosque was too small; construction was possible with the help of villagers and other benefactors. The main prayer hall is open on four sides and is decorated on all surfaces with the same gold and brown colour scheme as the domes. The mihrab has four rows of egg-shaped recesses set in a gold mosaic surface. The mosque has eight minarets and there is a plan to add another one to reach 150 m (492 ft). Both for the number of domes and the height of this minaret, the community hopes to be entered into *Guinness World Records*.

# 3

# Turkey & Central Asia

**TIMURID: AKSARAY MAUSOLEUM,
SAMARKAND, UZBEKISTAN** (1470s)

Built as the Timurid Empire was in decline, this small mausoleum was constructed because the Gur Emir Mausoleum – the dynastic tomb of the Timurids – had no more space for burial chambers. It was never finished; its exterior, for example, is completely unadorned. The interior decoration was done in the traditional Central Asian *kundal* style, by which a pattern or ornamentation was created in relief, which was then painted or gilded, creating a shimmering three-dimensional effect.

Monuments of Islamic architecture are nowadays often a source of great national pride, and justly so, but over the course of history, the regions in this chapter have been part of different empires, with large cities and important trade routes. Some of these cities, famous in their time, did not survive. For some time after Baghdad ceased to be the centre of learning in the Islamic world, and before Cairo and Córdoba rose to prominence, Konye-Urgench (in what is now Turkmenistan) was at the heart of Islamic civilization and learning. Avicenna, or Ibn Sina (980–1037), the father of modern medicine, lived there for a while. The scholar and scientist al-Biruni (973–1052) spent his first twenty-five years in the city. The mathematician and polymath al-Khwarizmi (*c.* 780–*c.* 850 CE) came from this region (his name is the source of the word 'algorithm'). In the 14th century, Ibn Battuta (1304–1368/9), the legendary scholar and explorer, rode into the bazaar of Konye-Urgench on horseback and became so stuck in the crowds that he could go neither forwards nor back. He wrote:

*It is the largest, greatest, most beautiful and most important city of the Turks. It has fine bazaars and broad streets, a great number of buildings and abundance of commodities; it shakes under the weight of its population, ... and is agitated by them like the waves of the sea.*

The city went through periods of prosperity and decline as the object of conquest by both Genghis Khan (who sacked it in 1221) and Timur (who destroyed it in 1388). The magnificent Turabek Khanum Mausoleum (see p. 156) and the tall Kutlug Timur minaret (see p. 156) give an indication of the grandeur of this city. It also had a famous Friday mosque, commissioned by Turabek Khanum, wife of Kutlug Timur (r. 1321–1336), of which nothing remains.

One of the most abundantly creative buildings in Turkey (and perhaps in all of Islamic architecture) is the 13th-century Great Mosque and Hospital of Divriği (see p. 117). It is now considered to be without precedent, though this might be because there is no other Mengujekid architecture left. The Mengujekid dynasty ruled from the city of Erzincan, but its location in an earthquake zone, in common with so many regions in Turkey and Central Asia, means that nothing of their architecture in this city has survived.

The architecture of Turkey and Central Asia has had a profound global influence. Many contemporary mosques, whether small or grand, look to the Ottoman architecture of Turkey for inspiration. Tall, pencil-shaped minarets, a large central dome, Ottoman-style calligraphic ornamentation on dome interiors: these are features that can be found in many contemporary mosques around the world. But there is much more to Ottoman architecture than just slim minarets and domes. Take, for example, a segment of a column in the 16th-century Behram Pasha Mosque in Diyarbakır (see p. 128), carved out of stone, resembling a woven, knotted intersection of bands – it is architecture made fluid. Why would the builders go to the trouble to make this? Did the client ask for this time-consuming small detail to be made? Was it the initiative of the chief architect, or of the mason? Something similar can be asked of the 17th-century Tilya-Kori Madrasa in Samarkand (see p. 145), where a coiled band of glazed ceramic tiles twists around an arched entrance, created with great skill in cylindrical, curved segments, painted by hand.

The architecture of Samarkand, Bukhara and more widely in Central Asia is an architecture of colour: glazed tiles and painted interiors demonstrate enormously sophisticated skill on the part of craftsmen, as well as an ability to execute concepts to very high standards of workmanship. There are so many details to marvel at. But, lest we romanticize too much, it is also the case that many of the artisans who built the magnificent monuments of Samarkand were brought there against their will by Timur after his conquests.

Highly sophisticated stone architecture and decoration is found especially in Anatolia (eastern Turkey) and Azerbaijan. The Anatolian Seljuk-era tombstones of Ahlat (see p. 117) are acknowledged as some of the most skilled examples of stone carving anywhere in the Islamic world, and it is clear that the artisans who

**OTTOMAN: TILES IN THE HALL OF THE ABLUTION FOUNTAIN, HAREM, TOPKAPI PALACE, ISTANBUL, TURKEY** (1668)
The Imperial Harem (see also p. 129) is renowned for its extraordinarily diverse and opulent use of glazed ceramic tiles: floor-to-ceiling, wall-to-wall. Installed when the Harem was renovated after a severe fire in 1666, most of them are the more well-known Iznik tiles, but there are also Kütayha tiles (such as these), made in the town of Kütayha.

**HAZRET SULTAN MOSQUE, NUR-SULTAN, KAZAKHSTAN** (2012)
The capital of Kazakhstan, Nur-Sultan (formerly Astana), a planned city, has become known for its grand architectural projects. Hazret Sultan Mosque, constructed between 2009 and 2012, is one of the largest mosques in Central Asia. Its four minarets are 77 m (253 ft) tall, and it can accommodate 10,000 worshippers. Inside and out, it is mostly white, and is ornately decorated in Kazakh style. It was named in honour of 12th-century Sufi poet Ahmed Yasawi (also known as Hazret Sultan, or Holy Sultan), who was born in Kazakhstan and for whom Timur commissioned a mausoleum (see p. 165).

carved these tombstones also applied their skills to buildings in the region. We can only wish more were known about them, as indeed about the builders and masons who worked in Nakhchivan in Azerbaijan in the 12th to 14th centuries. During this period, a number of mausolea were built that were unusual in their shape and exceptionally complex and sophisticated in their exterior decoration of baked (and sometimes glazed) brick. The geometric compositions on their façades are some of the most accomplished and daring in the history of Islamic geometric design.

As well as exploring the architecture and architectural details from some of the most familiar eras, such as the Ottoman (*c.* 1299–1922) and Timurid (*c.* 1370–1507), also included are buildings and stories that are much less well known, although this region has in fact received a great deal of attention from architectural historians. They have mapped out chronologies, influences and the evolution of architectural features and have demonstrated that Central Asia and Turkey (and adjoining regions) comprised a creatively dynamic and fluid region. Architectural ideas were adopted, developed and spread widely, as may be seen by the evidence of buildings that remain.

**SALTUKID: TOMB OF MELIKE MAMA HATUN, TERCAN, ERZINCAN, TURKEY** (13TH C)

Mama Hatun was the leader (*melike*, or queen) of the Saltukid dynasty between 1191 and 1200. Her tomb, surrounded by a ringed wall with an inner diameter of 13 m (42 ft 6 in), is one of the most remarkable architectural forms in Turkish architecture. The entrance portal is framed by complex geometrical compositions hewn in stone, and features a stone muqarnas composition with various geometric patterns on the individual faces. A stone calligraphic panel identifies the architect as Mufaddal the Cross-eyed, from Ahlat (famous for its tombstones with intricate geometric compositions; see p. 117).

## MENGUJEKID: GREAT MOSQUE AND HOSPITAL, DIVRIĞI, TURKEY (1229)

It is thought that the most splendid Mengujekid architecture would have been in the city of Erzincan, but its location in an earthquake zone means that nothing from Erzincan remains. Divriği was less important, but its Great Mosque and Hospital are now perhaps able to give an impression of what the Mengujekid monuments in Erzincan might have looked like. Turan Malik, daughter of longest-serving Mengujekid ruler Fakr al-Din Bahramshah, commissioned the hospital. The complex was completed just as the Anatolian Seljuks annexed almost all Mengujekid territory. An extra bit of text was chiselled into the foundation stone, acknowledging the dominance of the new masters. It is said that the shadow cast across the entrance resembles a man praying.

## ARTUQID: GREAT MOSQUE OF MARDIN, TURKEY (1176)

At an elevation of 1,300 m (4,265 ft), Mardin looks out over the vast plains of Upper Mesopotamia in Syria. Mardin's citadel has been notoriously impregnable: Saladin tried to take it, as did the Mongols. Timur was able to take the town but not the citadel. Artuqid ruler Qutb al-Din al-Ghazi commissioned the cylindrical stone minaret for the Great Mosque of Mardin to commemorate the start of his reign. At the base of the minaret is a beautifully designed and executed inscription in the angular and balanced square Kufic script.

## ANATOLIAN SELJUK: AHLAT TOMBSTONES, TURKEY (12TH–15TH C)

Ahlat is an ancient town in Turkey's Eastern Anatolia Region. It is known for its thousands of tombs from between the 12th and 15th centuries. There are six cemeteries, with the Seljuk-era Meydanlik cemetery having the most ornate tombstones. Some of the most skilled stone carving in Turkey, perhaps even in the Islamic world, can be found here. Ahlat and its craftsmen had an important influence on the architectural decoration in Turkey. The tombstones bear the name of the deceased, the name of the person who built the grave, and verses from the Quran. Front and back have different decorations and feature geometric designs and depictions of lamps, dragons and floral motifs.

**OPPOSITE & RIGHT**

## ANATOLIAN SELJUK: SULTANHANI CARAVANSERAI, AKSARAY, TURKEY (1229)

Seljuk Anatolia had approximately 250 caravanserais, of which this was the largest. Sultanhanı was built by a Syrian architect, Muhammad ibn Khalwan al-Dimashqi. Its front wall is 50 m (98 ft) wide. The 13 m (43 ft)-high main entrance *pishtaq* (opposite) has a beautiful stone muqarnas composition, framed by complex geometrical patterns carved in stone. In the middle of the main courtyard is a small free-standing kiosk-mosque (right), typical of Seljuk caravanserais. Elevated on arches, it is accessed via external stone stairs.

**ABOVE & RIGHT**

## ESHREFID: EŞREFOĞLU MOSQUE, BEYŞEHIR, TURKEY (1299)

Beyşehir was the capital of the Eshrefid beylik (Anatolian semi-independent principality) and a flourishing cultural centre; Eşrefoğlu is one of the few remaining wooden mosques from this era. The roof is supported by forty-two cedarwood columns, 7.5 m (24 ft 6 in) in length, and capped with painted wooden muqarnas capitals. In the central hall is a *karlik*, or large snow well, at least 3 m (10 ft) deep. In the winter snow would be shovelled off the roof into the well, where it was stored for use in the summer. The humidity created by the ice would have helped to preserve the wooden beams.

LEFT

### ANATOLIAN SELJUK: GÖK MADRASA, SIVAS, TURKEY (1271)

By the time this madrasa was built, the Anatolian Seljuks were no longer their own masters; they survived because their Mongol overlords let them. Three madrasas were built in Sivas in 1271, all commissioned by Seljuk vizier Sâhib Ata (see also below). It is thought that the style of the madrasa and its decoration gives clues as to how 13th-century Mongol buildings in Iran and eastern Asia might have looked (very few have survived). The name of the architect, Kaluyan al-Konavi, is carved on either side of the main entrance. It is one of the most ornate Anatolian Seljuk madrasas: the two minarets are made of brick and black and blue glazed tiles, the façade is a combination of large elements and incredibly detailed carved stone. Designed as a courtyard with four iwans, it used to be part of a much larger complex.

RIGHT

### ANATOLIAN SELJUK: INCE MINARELI MADRASA, KONYA, TURKEY (1265)

Commissioned, like the building shown above, by Seljuk vizier Sâhib Ata, one of the great builders of the Anatolian Seljuk era, the madrasa, unlike most other Seljuk madrasas, does not have a muqarnas composition over the entrance. Instead, it has an elaborate stone design that features interwoven bands of text and geometric and vegetal designs. By the time of its commission, the Seljuks were no longer independent, having been beaten on the battlefield by the Mongols in 1243. However, they still kept building and it is possible to detect a Mongol influence. The architect was Kölük bin Abdullah, who is thought to have worked on several other commissions by Sâhib Ata. *Ince minareli* means 'slender minaret'; a large part of the minaret collapsed at the beginning of the 20th century.

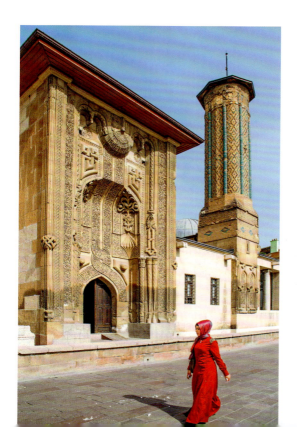

ABOVE & RIGHT

**ANATOLIAN SELJUK: WINGED ANGELS, KONYA CITADEL, TURKEY** (13TH C)

Up to the 19th century, Konya still had its city walls. Descriptions from visitors over the centuries make it clear that the walls were adorned with statues (including a colossal headless statue of Hercules, right next to the gate into the city) and 13th-century stone reliefs, such as the winged angels seen above. They were there to show the wealth and security of Konya and were thought to have talismanic, protective powers. A 19th-century drawing (right) shows a square gate block in Konya with an arched entrance, above which on either side are the winged angels, now in two different museum collections.

LEFT

**KARAMANID: MIHRAB FROM THE DAMSAKÖY TAŞKINPAŞA MOSQUE, CAPPADOCIA, TURKEY** (c. mid-14th c)

This mihrab is made entirely of walnut wood, carved with extraordinary craftsmanship and showing exceptional compositional skill. It measures 3.5 x 2 m (8 x 6 ft 6 in), and is framed by two bands of calligraphy with verses from the Quran. The keel arch and the smaller arch within have multiple borders of intricately carved vegetal designs. Above the arch is a twelvefold geometric star composition. The only wooden mihrab in Anatolia, it is now in the Ankara Ethnographic Museum.

RIGHT

**RUMI'S TOMB, KONYA, TURKEY** (1274)

The site of the tomb and other structures was originally a rose garden, a gift made in 1228 by the Seljuk sultan to Rumi's father, a theologian. The Persian poet and Sufi mystic Rumi was buried here, next to his father. The tombs of Rumi's son and other Sufi sheikhs were built around the grave. In 1369, the Karamanids built the conical, fluted turquoise tower that is now the most defining visual aspect of the tomb. The epitaph reads: 'When we are dead, seek not our tomb in the earth, but find it in the hearts of men.'

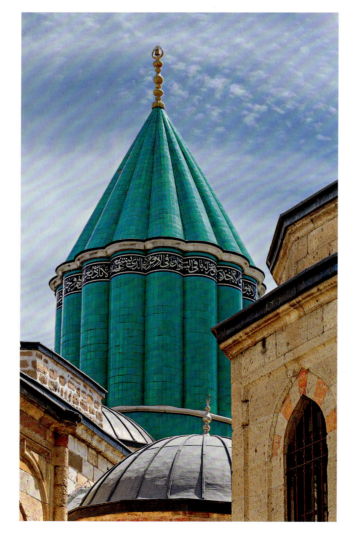

OPPOSITE

**OTTOMAN: GREAT MOSQUE OF BURSA, TURKEY** (1399)

Bursa was the first capital of the Ottomans. Its Great Mosque has twenty domes, all the same size and set out in a 5 x 4 grid. Underneath its central dome is an eighteen-sided marble *şadirvan* (fountain set in a pool), over which is a large opening in the roof that allows light to pour into the central space. The mosque's walnut minbar is one of the finest in all of Islam, beautifully made and very large. Designed by architect Ali Neccar, the mosque was financed by war booty after the Ottoman victory over the Crusader armies at Nicopolis.

LEFT

**OTTOMAN: ŠARENA MOSQUE, TETOVO, NORTH MACEDONIA** (1495)

Originally built in 1495, it was improved seventy years later on the initiative of the two daughters of the Ottoman pasha, Hoorshide and Mensoureh. It was rebuilt by Abdurrahman Pasha in 1833. The extremely elaborate and colourful painted decorations on the exterior and interior of the mosque date from this period. The painting is done in the secco technique, whereby a pigment is mixed with an organic binding agent (in this case, egg). It is said that 30,000 eggs were used to paint the entire mosque.

RIGHT

**OTTOMAN: EYÜP SULTAN MOSQUE, ISTANBUL, TURKEY** (1458)

Abu Ayyub al-Ansari, after whom the mosque is named, was a close companion of the Prophet Muhammad, as well as his standardbearer, and was killed in the first Arab siege of Constantinople (674–78 CE). The mosque complex contains a mausoleum marking his tomb, which attracts thousands of visitors each day; it is greatly venerated by Muslims and is Istanbul's most sacred site. The mausoleum is entirely covered in vibrant, colourful Iznik tiles, epitomizing the splendour of Ottoman art and architecture.

ABOVE & RIGHT

**OTTOMAN: BLUE MOSQUE, ISTANBUL, TURKEY** (1617)

Sultan Ahmed I was thirteen when he ascended the throne, and he reigned over a shrinking empire. To build a new imperial mosque in Istanbul without any military successes to his name, with public funds rather than the spoils of war, was controversial. Yet on completion it was considered to be the most beautiful of all sultanic mosques in Istanbul. Designed by chief imperial architect Mehmed Agha, it has six minarets, five main domes and eight secondary domes, and is known as the Blue Mosque because of the extensive use of glazed ceramic tiles from Iznik (its official name is the Sultan Ahmed Mosque). Ahmed died only three months after the inauguration of his mosque, at the age of twenty-seven.

**OTTOMAN: SELIMIYE MOSQUE, EDIRNE, TURKEY** (1575)

Designed by the Ottoman master architect and civil engineer Mimar Sinan when he was in his eighties, it is his great masterpiece and therefore also the great masterpiece of Ottoman architecture. Commissioned by Sultan Selim II, the mosque is part of a larger complex (*külliyesi*) that includes a madrasa, a primary school, a covered market and a house for the *muwaqqit* (the mosque's timekeeper). The mosque is especially remarkable for the organization of its interior space, and shows Sinan's profound mastery over the creation of an experiential environment that evokes spirituality and inspires awe.

**OTTOMAN: BIRDHOUSE, YENI VALIDE MOSQUE, ÜSKÜDAR, ISTANBUL, TURKEY** (1710)

On the sun-facing sides of mosques and houses in Turkey, birdhouses can often be found. The Ottomans traditionally built these structures for small birds such as sparrows, swallows and goldfinches. They are often elaborate multistorey structures, designed to look like mosques or palaces. Helping out small creatures was seen as *sevap* – a good deed, to gain favour with God. They also served to elicit compassion in others for God's creation.

**OTTOMAN: BEHRAM PASHA MOSQUE, DIYARBAKIR, TURKEY** (1572)

Designed by the great imperial architect Mimar Sinan, the mosque is covered almost entirely in alternating black and white ashlar stone courses. Inside, Iznik tiles decorate the lower parts of the walls. The columns around the courtyard have complex knotted inserted sections. Above the entrance is an extraordinary muqarnas composition, where the surfaces of the muqarnas elements have all been carved in a herringbone motif. This mosque shows Ottoman architectural design at its most innovatively creative.

**OTTOMAN: DOUBLE SHUTTERS IN THE ABLUTION FOUNTAIN HALL, HAREM, TOPKAPI PALACE, ISTANBUL, TURKEY** (1668)

The Harem was the part of Topkapı Palace where the sultan and his extended family lived. It has more than 400 rooms, arranged around courtyards. The central panels in these wooden shutters are fivefold compositions: in the middle is a tenfold star design, on the corners are quarter-tenfold stars. In between is where the craftsmen could express their creativity. Mother-of-pearl, tortoiseshell and bone were typically used for compositions such as these. The Topkapı Palace had its own workshops for most craftworkers: jewellers, book makers, armourers, woodworkers and many more. Together they were known as Ehl-i Hiref (The Community of the Talented).

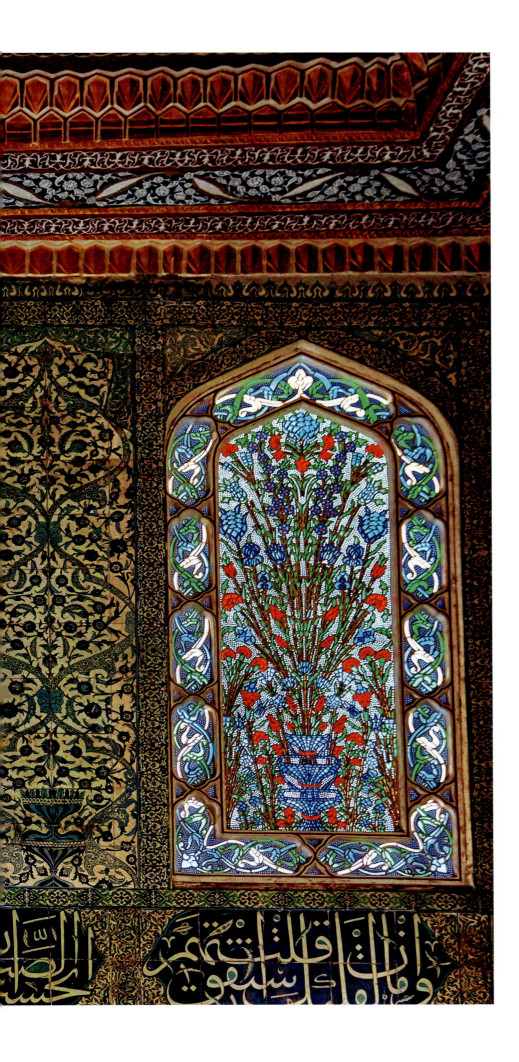

**OTTOMAN: TWIN KIOSKS / APARTMENT OF THE CROWN PRINCE, TOPKAPI PALACE, ISTANBUL, TURKEY** (1600)

These two rooms in the Imperial Harem date from around 1600, although the palace was built in the 15th century. Male relatives of the sultan competing for the throne were a threat to the Ottoman Empire. These opulent apartments were part of the *kafes* ('cage') system, where would-be heirs were locked up for years to prevent them from claiming the throne. When Süleyman II ascended to the throne in 1687, he had spent forty-six years in the *kafes* of Topkapı Palace. The beautiful windows are made of stucco inlaid with glass pieces. First, a wooden frame was made into which plaster was poured. A design was carved out of the dried plaster and glass pieces were placed, from the back. It could take almost a year to make one such window and the risk of damaging the fragile plaster was constantly present.

LEFT

### IREMIT MOSQUE, MARAL, ARTVIN PROVINCE, TURKEY (1851)

This mosque is built with chestnut wood and the interior decorations are mostly in walnut. Maral is located in the remote Macahel valley, close to Turkey's border with Georgia. There are several other unique wooden mosques in the valley. Although built in the Ottoman era, the mosque is very much a local design, constructed and embellished by the village. The red paint on the interior is made by the villagers, using traditional rose madder pigment.

OPPOSITE

### SHEIKH HAMZA ZAFIR TOMB, ERTUĞRUL TEKKE, YILDIZ, ISTANBUL, TURKEY (1905)

The Libyan Sufi Sheikh Zafir was the spiritual and political adviser to Ottoman sultan Abdülhamid II for more than thirty years. His tomb, sited in the Ertuğrul Tekke Mosque complex, was built by the sultan's chief palace architect, Raimondo D'Aronco. D'Aronco introduced Art Nouveau architecture to Istanbul and sought to combine Islamic architecture with other architectural styles that were popular at the time. The sheikh's tomb combines the curvilinear shapes of Jugendstil (German and Austrian Art Nouveau) architecture with traditional elements of Ottoman tomb design.

OVERLEAF

### SAKIRIN MOSQUE, ISTANBUL, TURKEY (2009)

Often called Turkey's most modern mosque, this is the first mosque whose interior was designed by a woman – Zeynep Fadıllıoğlu (the architect was Hüsrev Tayla). It was built in memory of Semiha and Ibrahim Sakir, a well-known Turkish philanthropist couple, by their children. The mosque features a large, prominent balcony as the prayer space for women and, unconventionally, women enter the mosque through the main door, as the men do. The mosque has two minarets, a dome made out of aluminium composite, and an acrylic minbar; it also has a space for art exhibitions.

ABOVE

**TOMB COMPLEX OF SOMUNCU BABA, DARENDE, TURKEY** (17TH C/20TH C)
Located in a scenic gorge in eastern Turkey, this tomb complex attracts over 800,000 visitors a year. Sheikh Hamid-i Vali, better known as Somuncu Baba, was a 14th-century teacher of Islam, revered as a saint. He gave the first Friday sermon in the Great Mosque of Bursa, immediately after it was completed (see p. 122). His tomb is in a 17th-century mosque; next to it is a new mosque, which features an enormous wooden ceiling designed as a radiating eight-pointed star.

ABOVE

**SANCAKLAR MOSQUE, ISTANBUL,
TURKEY** (2013)

Set on sloping terrain in an Istanbul suburb,
often only the flat roof and minaret are
visible, depending on where you stand. The
architect, Emre Arolat, deliberately sought
to focus on the essence of religious space
and not engage in discussions around
form. Constructed of light-grey stone and
reinforced concrete, it blurs the boundaries
between man-made and natural. The central
prayer hall has a stepped floor, and women
pray next to men rather than separated
from them. The shape of the ceiling gives
the prayer hall the appearance of a cave.
Unusually for a mosque, especially in Turkey,
it has no dome.

**SAMANID: TOMB OF THE SAMANIDS, BUKHARA, UZBEKISTAN** (LATE 9TH TO EARLY 10TH C CE)

The family mausoleum of the Samanids, this is one of the earliest tombs in the Islamic world, and resembles a Zoroastrian fire temple. It is a slightly tapering cube, measuring almost 10 m (33 ft) per side, with a hemispherical dome on top. Made of baked bricks that have been arranged in such a way to give it a basket-weave appearance, it is one of the earliest buildings to feature squinches as a solution to the problem of how to transition from the square walls of a building to the circular base of a dome.

**CHAGATAI-KHAN: MAUSOLEUM OF BUYAN-QULI KHAN, BUKHARA, UZBEKISTAN** (1358)

The mausoleum of Buyan-Quli, ruler of the Chagatai, contains some of the finest carved terracotta pieces, glazed in various shades of blue. Calligraphy is framed in lavender-indigo, white, blue and manganese (which almost looks black); the light-blue glaze has a hint of green. The photograph shows one of the spandrels – no join lines are visible and it is therefore possible that this huge piece would have been fired in a kiln in its entirety.

**TIMURID: SHAH-I-ZINDA NECROPOLIS, SAMARKAND, UZBEKISTAN** (14TH–15TH C)

Shah-i-Zinda ('the living king') refers to Qusam bin Abbas, a cousin of the Prophet Muhammad, who is buried here. The complex is essentially a long, narrow avenue lined with mausolea, most of them built between 1360 and 1436 for the Timurid elite. Many of the sites are associated with women of the Timurid court, and the magnificence and overwhelming beauty of this complex with its exquisite tilework was created mostly through female patronage. Timur's principal wives, his sisters and his wet-nurse are all buried here.

Over the entrance to the tomb of Shirin Biga Aga, one of Timur's sisters, is a calligraphic text quoting Socrates on the hard nature of life and the constant agony of being separated from loved ones. It comes from an important and popular 11th-century book, Mubassir's *Choicest Maxims* (one of the first books to be printed in the English language, incidentally).

**TIMURID: REGISTAN, SAMARKAND, UZBEKISTAN** (1420–1659)
Measuring 60 x 110 m (200 x 360 ft), the Registan was the main square at the heart of Samarkand. In the 14th century, Timur built a covered shopping street from one city gate to the other, with the Registan in the middle, but over the centuries it has changed. Three madrasas face on to the square, each spectacularly adorned with glazed clay tiles predominantly in azure and blue; from left to right: Ulugh Beg Madrasa (1420), Tilya-Kori Madrasa (1659; see p. 145) and Sher-Dor Madrasa (1636).

OPPOSITE

**SHAYBANID: TILYA-KORI MADRASA, SAMARKAND, UZBEKISTAN (1659)**

The Tilya-Kori Madrasa became Samarkand's congregational mosque when the collapsed Bibi Khanum Mosque could no longer fulfil that function. Its enormous courtyard is surrounded on three sides by study and sleeping cells for students. On the remaining side is a large prayer hall with adjacent chambers that make it large enough for Friday prayers. 'Tilya-Kori' means 'gold work', and refers to the gilded *kundal* relief painting (see p. 111) of its prayer hall. It is one of the three main buildings on the Registan square (see p. 143) and was the last to be built.

ABOVE

**SHAYBANID: BARAK KHAN MADRASA, TASHKENT, UZBEKISTAN (16TH C)**

After replacing the Timurids, the Shaybanids appointed Barak Khan as governor of Tashkent. His father was buried in a mausoleum with an attached *khanqah* (Sufi lodge), next to a mausoleum for an unknown cleric. In the 1550s, Barak Khan joined up the buildings and added a madrasa, creating a single unified façade with a large *pishtaq* in the centre, flanked by two domes on high drums. The madrasa is part of the Hast Imam Complex, which also includes a library that houses the world's oldest Quran, compiled in Medina during the reign of Caliph Uthman in 651 CE, nineteen years after the death of the Prophet Muhammad.

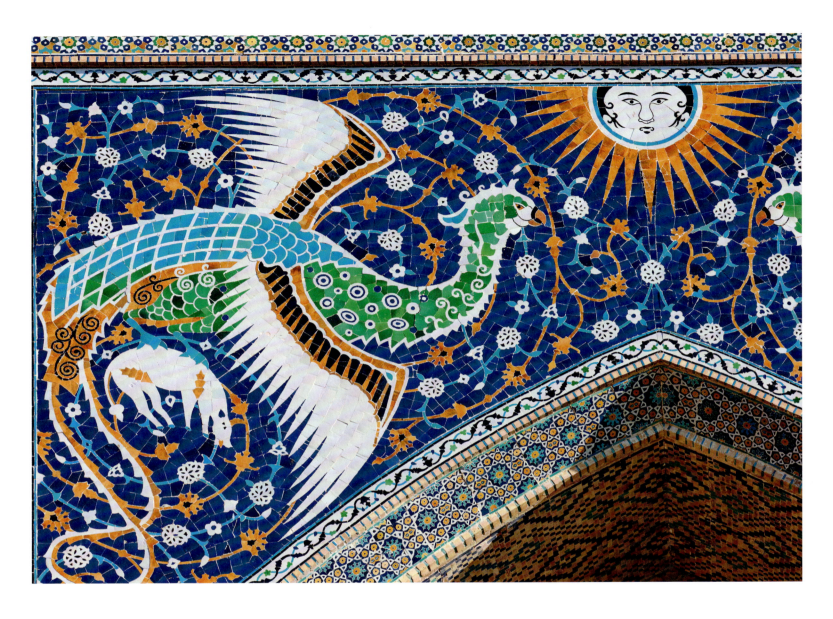

ABOVE

**JANID: MADRASA OF NADIR DIVAN-BEGI,
BUKHARA, UZBEKISTAN** (1623)

Bukhara used to have many ponds (*hauz*)
dotted around the city. One of these
is surrounded on three sides by the
Lyab-i Hauz ensemble, a trio of buildings
comprising the Kukeldash Madrasa (1569),
the Khanqah of Nadir Divan-begi (1620)
and the Madrasa of Nadir Divan-begi.
The most remarkable aspect of the
madrasa is the very large cut-ceramic
tile compositions on the spandrels of the
entrance portal arch. They depict two birds
(probably the mythical Persian *simurgh*)
facing a solar disc with a face. Both birds
are holding a deer in their claws.

OPPOSITE

**KHANATE OF KHIVA: KALTA MINAR,
KHIVA, UZBEKISTAN** (1855)

This unfinished minaret, commissioned by
the ruler of Khiva, Muhammad Amin Khan,
was intended to be 70 m (230 ft) tall, which
was believed to be high enough to see
Bukhara, 400 km (250 miles) away (although
this would have required an elevation of
12,000 m / 39,400 ft). Building stopped at
only 26 m (85 ft), on the death of the khan.
The minaret is adorned with glazed bricks in
geometric patterns in the characteristic blue,
green, yellow and white colours of Khiva.

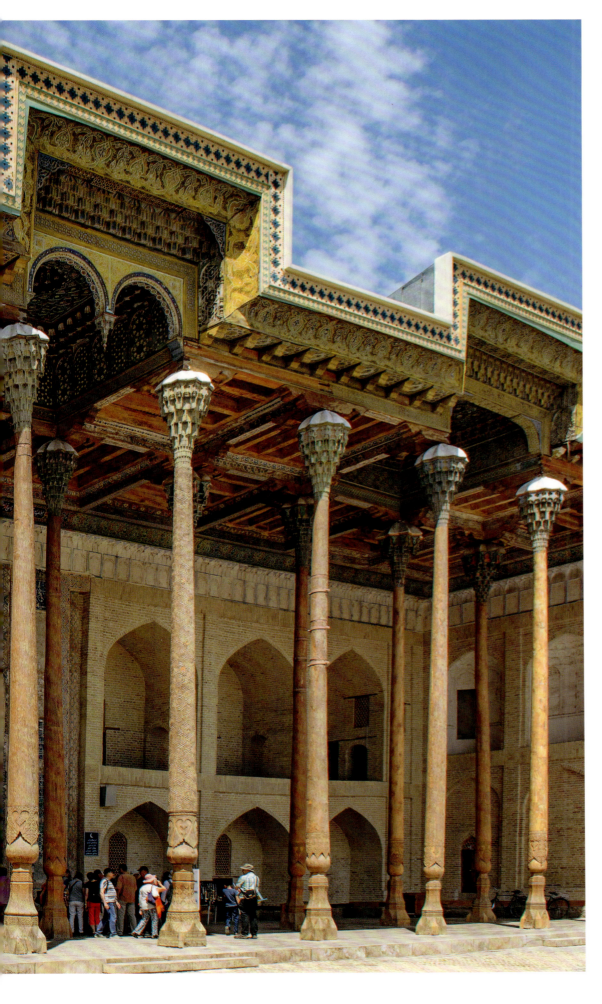

## JANID: BOLO HAUZ MOSQUE, BUKHARA, UZBEKISTAN (1712)

Although built as a Friday mosque, this was in practice used as the personal mosque of the ruling khan, who would walk from his home in the famous Ark Fortress across the square, his route completely covered in carpets. The painted wooden ceilings and supporting columns of the iwan are some of the most beautiful in Central Asia. Bukhara has extreme temperatures and the mosque was built to take this into account. Its central winter mosque, with thick walls, can be closed off and kept warm. In the summer, when temperatures are very high, the east-facing iwan brings in cool air.

**GUMBAZ SYNAGOGUE, SAMARKAND, UZBEKISTAN** (1891)

The main central space of this working synagogue, built by Uzbek craftsmen, is circular and covered by a dome (*gumbaz*). The synagogue's dedication plaque in Hebrew reads: 'The synagogue was erected by the will and at the expense of Rabbi Rafael bin Moshe Nosi Kalontar in memory of his wife Tsipora.' It was only after the Russian conquest of Central Asia in the second half of the 19th century that the Jewish communities of Samarkand, Bukhara and elsewhere were allowed to rebuild their old synagogues or build new ones.

### INAQID/KHANATE OF KHIVA: TASH HAULI PALACE, KHIVA, UZBEKISTAN (1838)

This extensive palace complex, built by the Khivan ruler Alla Kuli Khan, has two smaller courtyards, and a very large harem courtyard. Double-height iwans face north to catch the cool northerly winds in summer. The walls are faced with superb ceramic tile decorations in the traditional blue, turquoise and white colours of Khiva. The tilework was done by the brothers Abdallah and Ibadallah Jinn. The wooden ceilings of the iwans around the courtyards are adorned with geometric compositions, floral designs and calligraphy in golden-red colour schemes. Intricate carvings in the finest Khwarazm woodcarving tradition can be seen in the wooden columns and doors.

RIGHT

**NOH GUMBAD MOSQUE, BALKH, AFGHANISTAN** (8TH–9TH C CE)

This small mosque measures just 20 x 20 m (65 x 65 ft). It originally had nine brick domes; now only four columns and one arch remain, giving an insight into the mixing of pre-existing Sasanian decorative styles and developing Islamic styles. The building is covered in detailed vine leaves, vine scrolls, fir cones and palmettes, in carved stucco. It would once have been painted brightly.

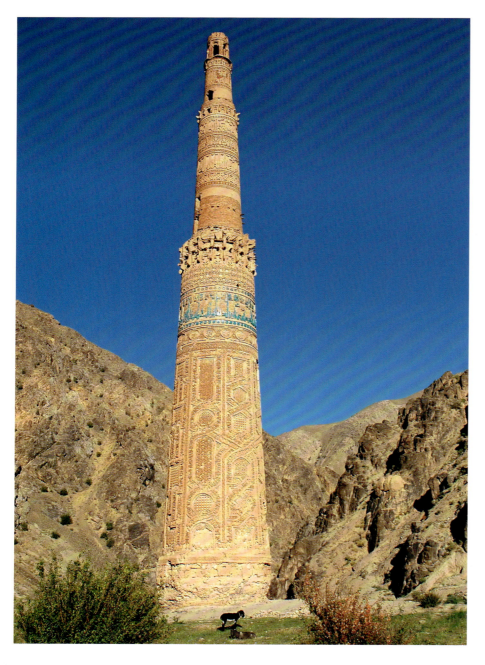

LEFT

**GHURID: MINARET OF JAM, AFGHANISTAN** (LATE 12TH C)

One of Afghanistan's most famous monuments, this enormous minaret stands in complete isolation in a rocky valley. Built entirely of baked brick, it is 65 m (213 ft) tall and is elaborately decorated with calligraphy, brick patterns, stucco and glazed bricks. The entire text of surah 19 of the Quran, Surah Maryam, is reproduced on the exterior, along with other inscriptions. It is generally accepted that the minaret is all that remains of Firozkoh, the summer capital of the Ghurid dynasty, and it is thought to have been the inspiration for the Qutb Minar in Delhi (see p. 65).

OPPOSITE

**GHAZNAVID: MINARET OF MASUD III, GHAZNI, AFGHANISTAN** (12TH C)

Nineteenth-century drawings show that the minaret was originally more than twice as tall as its current 20 m (66 ft) height, with a now-lost cylindrical upper half. In the background of the photograph is another minaret, that of Masud III's son and successor, Bahram Shah, built less than fifty years later. The external decoration on the father's minaret is much more detailed, with eight decorative bands of panels on its façades. These are filled with brick patterns and carved terracotta inscriptions, and floral designs and interlaced geometric motifs. Both minarets are designed in plan as eight-pointed stars.

**GHURID: FRIDAY MOSQUE OF HERAT, AFGHANISTAN** (EARLY 13TH C)

Built on the site of a previous mosque, Herat's Friday mosque was constructed entirely of brick, with three iwans on the central courtyard and a large dome over the area in front of the mihrab. Seven hundred years later, and despite the fact that Timur's wife Gawhar Shad built a new Friday mosque in 1417 outside the old city, the old mosque is still the heart of Herat. It has undergone much renovation, and the lavish glazed tiles in Timurid style are part of an ongoing restoration project begun in the 1940s.

LEFT & BELOW LEFT

**TURABEK KHANUM MAUSOLEUM, KONYE-URGENCH, TURKMENISTAN** (2ND HALF 14TH C)
One of the most exquisitely decorated buildings in all of Islamic architecture, this mausoleum has an interior covered in thousands of pieces of glazed ceramic tiles in colours not seen anywhere else (red, gold, brown, grass green, bright yellow). The tiled interior of the dome depicts a stylized view of the heavens, with tessellated forms including stars and pentagons, and a variety of floral and vegetal details. The exterior would also have been completely covered in glazed ceramics. The date of construction is unclear; it is possible that it was commissioned by Timur himself. See p. 318 for more information on Turabek Khanum and the legend around this mausoleum.

OPPOSITE

**ILKHANID: GUDI KHATUN MAUSOLEUM, GARABAGHLAR, AZERBAIJAN** (1338)
The mausoleum complex was built in honour of Gudi Khatun, wife of Hülegü Khan, grandson of Genghis Khan and founder of the Ilkhanid dynasty. The exterior is made of twelve half-cylinders covered in diagonal patterns of glazed and unglazed bricks, creating a square Kufic calligraphic composition. Inside are two chambers, the lower a vaulted crypt. The tower originally had a conical roof, probably also decorated in glazed and unglazed bricks.

RIGHT

**KHWARAZMIAN: KUTLUG TIMUR MINARET, KONYE-URGENCH, TURKMENISTAN** (11TH C TO 1336)
Visible from many kilometres away, the minaret is 62 m (203 ft) tall and 12 m (39 ft) in diameter at its base, tapering to 2 m (6 ft 6 in) at the top. Construction began in the early 11th century but was not completed until 300 years later during the reign of Kutlug Timur. The entrance to the minaret is several metres off the ground because it used to be accessed via the roof of the Friday mosque to which it belonged (commissioned by Kutlug Timur's wife, Turabek Khanum, and since destroyed). It originally had a platform at the top and may also have served as a watchtower and beacon. Turabek Khanum's mausoleum is visible near the minaret (see also images above).

The palace was built as a summer residence for the rulers of the Shaki Khanate by architect Haji Zeynalabdin Shirazi. Set at the foot of the Caucasus mountains, the two-storey palace has a noticeably symmetrical façade. It has large wooden windows over two floors in the middle, filled with stained glass from France. The wooden frames are from Russia. Inside are mirror-glass muqarnas compositions from Iran.

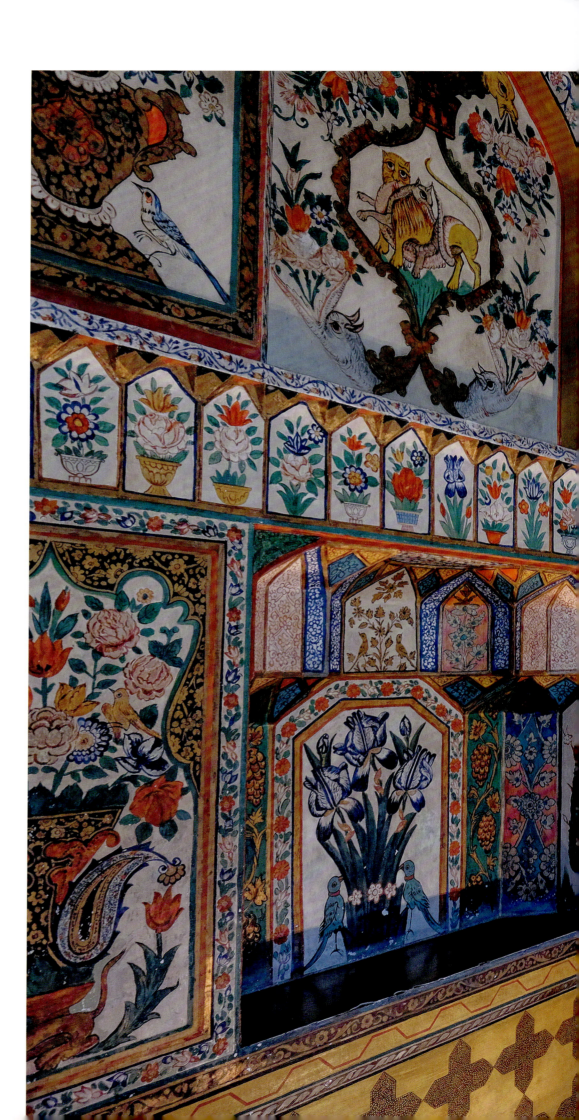

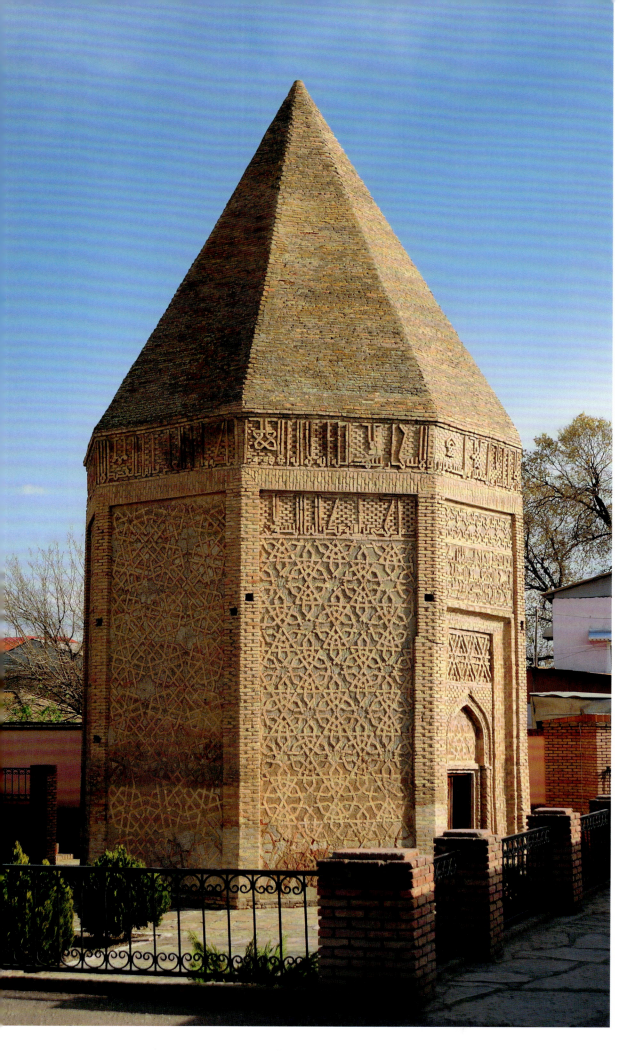

LEFT

**MAUSOLEUM OF YUSUF IBN KUSAYR, NAKHCHIVAN, AZERBAIJAN** (1162)

Azerbaijan in the 12th century produced some of the most complex and accomplished geometrical compositions and structures in Islamic architecture. This octagonal mausoleum, designed by renowned architect Ajami ibn Abubakr Nakhchivani, made in baked brick, is a prime example. Ajami was somewhat like the Mimar Sinan of 12th-century Azerbaijan: he built palaces, Friday mosques, madrasas, mausolea and government buildings. His signature on buildings became increasingly large and prominent. He created a design legacy that is sometimes referred to as the Nakhchivani school of architecture.

ABOVE
### SHEIKH MUSLIHIDDIN COMPLEX, KHUJAND, TAJIKISTAN (11TH–14TH C)

Sheikh Muslihiddin ruled Khujand – one of the oldest cities in Central Asia and an important trading hub – in the 12th century and was known as a holy man who could perform miracles. Over the centuries, his mausoleum has been rebuilt several times. It became a mausoleum-*khanqah*, and over the centuries a mosque and minaret have been added. More recently, the Sheikh Muslihiddin Madrasa has been built, with its bright blue-green dome made of lozenge-shaped scales.

BELOW
### MAZAR OF MUHAMMAD BASHARA, MAZAR-E SHARIF, TAJIKISTAN (1362)

Set on the bank of a small river, and cut into a mountainous slope, this small, domed tomb structure (*mazar*) has some of the most delicate carved terracotta decoration in Central Asia. The arched entrance is framed with calligraphic bands in glazed terracotta and columns in carved terracotta with an enormous variety of design elements and geometric patterns. All is framed by, and interspersed with, blue and turquoise majolica glazed bricks and glazed calligraphy. Nothing is known of Muhammad Bashara, but his tomb is a site of pilgrimage.

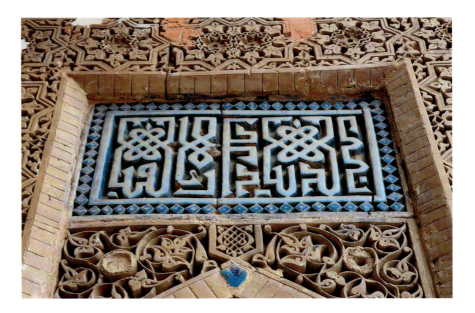

RIGHT

## QARAKHANID: BURANA TOWER, CHÜY VALLEY, KYRGYZSTAN (c. 11TH C)

Once 40 m (130 ft) tall, this ancient minaret is all that remains of the important Silk Road city of Balasagun, capital of the powerful Qarakhanid Empire between the 10th and 14th centuries. The entrance to the minaret is a couple of metres above ground because it was once attached to the Friday Mosque of Balasagun. The minaret and its brickwork patterns served as a template for many other minarets in Iran and Central Asia.

BELOW

## ISMA'ILI JAMATKHANA AND CENTRE, KHOROG, TAJIKISTAN (2018)

At the foot of the Pamir Mountains and on the shore of the fast-flowing Gunt River, this complex was created for the Isma'ili community (Jamat) in Tajikistan. The central entrance references local Pamir architecture as well as the poplar trees in the area: tall wooden pillars support a protruding roof, creating a huge open and welcoming façade. The wooden ceiling of the prayer hall is supported by five wooden columns and consists of rotating squares inside squares, decreasing in size, as is typical for Pamir homes. Local granite has been used for much of the interior and exterior walls, as well as the floors. It was designed by Farouk Noormohamed, Principal, FNDA Architecture.

OPPOSITE

## QARAKHANID: AISHA BIBI MAUSOLEUM, TARAZ, KAZAKHSTAN (11TH–12TH C)

Completely covered in an enormous variety of patterned terracotta tiles, the mausoleum was built by a Qarakhanid ruler in remembrance of Aisha Bibi, the girl he wanted to marry but whose parents forbade it. As she was secretly travelling to meet him, Aisha Bibi was bitten by a snake and died. The original 12th-century terracotta tiles stayed on the exterior for centuries because they were more like the ends of tapering bricks, deeply cemented into the 80 cm (30 in)-thick walls. The monument is associated with enduring love and is now a popular venue for wedding photos.

LEFT & ABOVE

**TIMURID: MAUSOLEUM OF KHOJA AHMED YASAWI, TURKISTAN, KAZAKHSTAN** (1405)

Ahmed Yasawi was a 12th-century poet and Sufi mystic who brought Sufism to Central Asia and made it accessible by writing mystical poetry in the Turkic language. Timur commissioned a new mausoleum to replace a smaller 12th-century one. Construction started in 1389 but remained unfinished when Timur died in 1405. Nonetheless, it is now one of the best-preserved Timurid monuments.

OVERLEAF

**ZHARKENT MOSQUE, ZHARKENT, KAZAKHSTAN** (1886)

The mosque was paid for with donations from the Uyghur community on the initiative of a local businessman, who wanted a building constructed from wood and without the use of nails. The architect was Chinese and his influence is seen throughout the building. The decorative themes are diverse: interior wooden beams are decorated with colourful Chinese-style clouds, and there are painted images of birds, fish and plants. The wooden minbar is free-standing in the centre of the prayer hall, and has a huge wooden Chinese-style canopy, as well as fluid Chinese paintings on the side. The entrance building looks like a typical Central Asian mosque or madrasa, with a large central *pishtaq* (entrance) and walls with arches extending on both sides. On top, a tiered wooden Chinese pagoda is in fact the minaret.

# 4
# Africa

The Islamic architecture of North Africa is much better known than that of the rest of the continent. Within the architecture of North Africa, Morocco is always very well represented, with its amazing Marinid madrasas in Fes and Marrakech, decorated with geometric tile compositions, carved stucco and carved wood. The Kutubiyya Mosque in Marrakech (see opposite) is named after the many booksellers in the souk surrounding the mosque (*koutoub* means 'book'). The Saadian Tombs in Marrakech (see p. 179) were forgotten about for centuries until a French plane flying over the city in the early 20th century to take photographs revealed their existence. Tunisia is the home of Kairouan, the fourth-holiest city in Islam, after Mecca, Medina and Jerusalem. Its Great Mosque (see pp. 182–83) tells the story of early Islam, of the links between Baghdad and Ifriqiya (the historical region comprising present-day Tunisia, eastern Algeria and western Libya). Tunisia was also the home of Ibn Khaldun (1332–1406), the great 14th-century historian whose influential book the *Muqaddimah* presented the world in a new light, observing and commenting on history, society, politics, social behaviour, theology and much more. The island of Djerba (see p. 184) is also part of Tunisia, thought to be the island of the lotus-eaters in Homer's *Odyssey*, whose fortified mosques tell a story of adaptation to external threats. Some of the buildings selected for Algeria happen to have a strong connection with modernist architecture. The Ibadi architecture of the M'zab Valley influenced modernist architect Le Corbusier; the large white exterior walls with small apertures do indeed look, if not modern, at least completely

**ALMOHAD: KUTUBIYYA MOSQUE, MARRAKECH, MOROCCO** (1147/1158?)
For a period of at least thirty years in the late 12th century there were two almost identical Kutubiyya mosques next to each other. Both were built by the Almohad ruler Abd-al-Mu'min, but it is not conclusively understood why. The first mosque had a retractable *maqsura* (an enclosed space for the sultan) and minbar, both designed by engineer al-Hajj Ya'ish of Malaga. The weight of the imam as he walked towards the minbar would activate a mechanical system that caused the minbar to move forward into the prayer hall. Similarly, weight-activated wooden screens would rise up out of the floor to create a *maqsura* as the sultan entered the mosque through a private underground corridor.

separate from other Islamic architecture in the region. The Ibadis in Algeria, like those in Djerba, sought to isolate themselves, and this had an impact on their architecture (see p. 186). When the president of Algeria asked Spanish architect Ricardo Bofill to design a new village in the desert (see p. 191), he received an amazing minimalist interpretation of Islamic architecture (although Bofill took his inspiration more from Persian than North African architecture).

Directly south of the North African region are such countries as Mauritania, Mali and Niger. Connections between North and Central/West Africa were along trade routes. In the 9th and 10th centuries, North African Muslim merchants already travelled across the Sahara to do business in the Empire of Ghana (in present-day Mauritania and Mali). Chinguetti in Mauritania sat at the centre of various trans-Saharan trade routes. For centuries, it was one of the most important cities in Northwest Africa, not just for commerce but also for religion. It was a staging post for Muslims on their way to Mecca, as well as a destination in itself for those who were not able to go to Mecca. It was an important centre of Islamic learning – at its peak it had thirty libraries. The Chinguetti Mosque (see right) is considered to be the national symbol of Mauritania.

The manner in which Islam came to West Africa is very different from how it came to East Africa. In West Africa, it came mostly via the trans-Saharan trade routes, while in East Africa it was mostly Arab seafaring traders who gradually brought the cultural and religious customs to the Swahili coast. There are still a great many stories to tell about Islamic architecture in West Africa: this chapter makes a start. The story of the Great Mosque of Porto-Novo (see p. 208) in Benin is extraordinary: its appearance was determined by descendants of freed Muslim slaves returning from Brazil in the 19th century. The Portuguese style of building that

**CHINGUETTI MOSQUE, MAURITANIA**
(13TH–14TH C)
The desert town of Chinguetti connected the Mediterranean with sub-Saharan Africa for over 1,000 years. In its heyday, it could have around 30,000 camels within its city limits, from caravans coming and going. The mosque and minaret are built from unmortared stone. Its prayer room has four aisles and a mihrab with two arches.

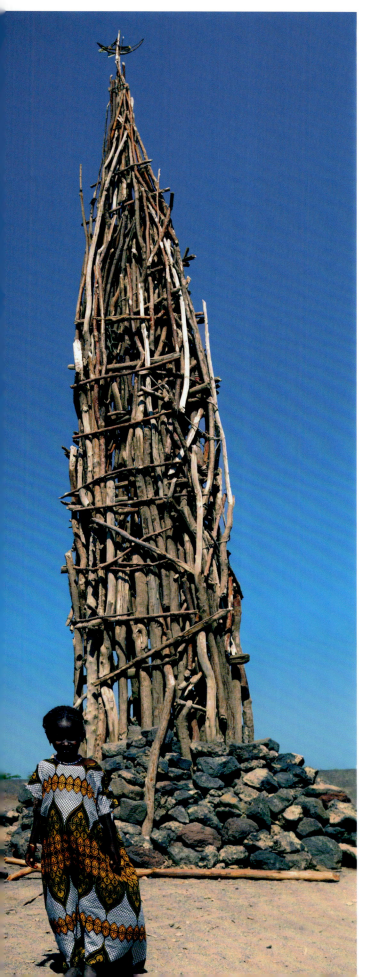

they had learned in Brazil influenced the architecture of mosques that they then built in Benin, which more than a hundred years later is now typical mosque architecture in Benin and surrounding countries. Other examples include the strange story of the seven mosques in the town of Bani, Burkina Faso, all built within a period of two years (see p. 204); or the remarkable adobe mosques around the town of Kouto in northern Ivory Coast (see p. 204); or the story of the favourite architect of the Sokoto Caliphate in 19th-century Nigeria, Babban Gwani, who was said to build only at night, on his own. He built numerous palaces and mosques in northern Nigeria. Many of his descendants are builders and it is said that if your house has not been built by a descendant of Babban Gwani, it is as if your house has not been built at all. So many stories, so little academic research!

The East African coast has for millennia been part of a maritime network, visited by traders from India, Arabia, Iran, China and South-East Asia. The city-state of Kilwa Kisiwani in Tanzania was one of the most important and prosperous in the region, its mosque built of coral stone. In the 19th century, the Sultan of Oman moved his court from Muscat (in Oman) to Stone Town (capital of Zanzibar, off the coast of Tanzania).

Ethiopia, Sudan and Somalia, by their proximity to Arabia (Sudan is just across the Red Sea from Mecca), were the first countries outside Arabia to receive Islam. The mosque of Fakhr al-Din in Somalia (see p. 199) is one of Africa's earliest mosques; Ibn Battuta prayed there on his visit in the 14th century. Obtaining a photograph of it has proven to be a big challenge, as it has for many other parts of Africa: the rich history of Islam in Africa is currently not reflected in the textual and visual documentation available. This chapter can perhaps play a small start in redressing this.

**HAJI HABIB MOSQUE, ASSAITA, AFAR, ETHIOPIA** (2007)
Assaita is a town in the northeast of Ethiopia. The mosque was built along the road to Assaita with wood brought by nomads passing through with their camels. There are examples of other mosques built in this way in the area. They rely on regular maintenance and often do not have a long life.

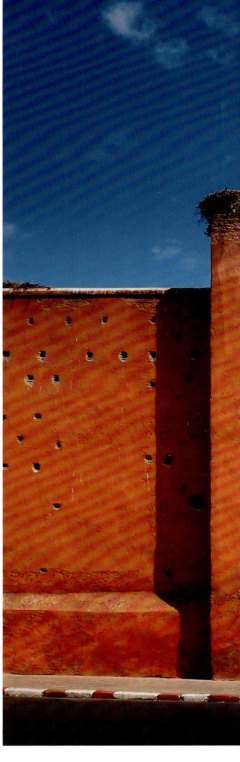

**ALMORAVID: BAYRUDIYYIN DOME, MARRAKECH, MOROCCO** (c. 1125)

This is part of the now-destroyed Almoravid mosque complex, which covered a large area of approximately 80 x 120 m (260 x 395 ft). After the Almohads came to power, they took issue with what they considered the faulty orientation of the mosque and replaced it with a new one, the Ben Youssef Mosque. What remains of the Almoravid mosque are the ablution facilities, of which the structure of the dome is a part. This small building has the first extant presence of muqarnas in North Africa.

**ALMOHAD: BAB AGNAOU, MARRAKECH, MOROCCO** (1147)

Designed as a giant horseshoe arch, this is the public entrance to the citadel (*kasbah*) and royal palace complex of Marrakech. It is the most embellished part of the fortifications of Marrakech. The area around the entrance arch is covered in stone, mostly blue-grey in colour, from nearby Gueliz, contrasting with the red stone of the city walls. Above the concentric carved arch elements are delicately carved shallow curvilinear leaf designs. A wide Quranic inscription carved in stone borders the arch on three sides.

LEFT

**MARINID: CARVED AND PAINTED
WOODEN PANEL, MOROCCO** (14TH C)
In Marinid buildings, carved wooden panels
such as this were typically placed near the
ceiling, above stucco panels. The repeated
Arabic text in this panel spells 'good luck',
written forward and in mirror image.
Measuring 48 x 303 cm (19 x 121 in), it is
thought to have come from a madrasa in Fes.

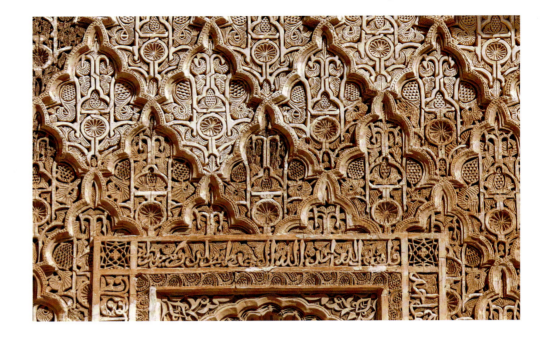

**BELOW**

**MARINID: BOU INANIA MADRASA, FES, MOROCCO** (1355)

The central courtyard of the madrasa is surrounded by students' rooms, the prayer hall and two domed halls. Beauty can be seen in all directions. There are ceramic dados with a wide range of complex and innovative geometric compositions; finely carved stucco above and on the columns and arches; intricately carved and constructed wooden panels, doors, ceilings and window screens. The floors are tiled with geometric patterns. It can be considered the high point of Marinid architecture and design.

**SAADI: BEN YOUSSEF MADRASA, MARRAKECH, MOROCCO** (1565)

One of the very few Moroccan madrasas built after the reign of the Marinids, it is an almost perfect square (42 x 42 m / 138 x 138 ft). A long covered corridor takes a visitor into the courtyard, with a shallow pool in the middle. Student accommodation is arranged around seven small double-height courtyards, connected via a perimeter corridor. This unusual arrangement greatly increased capacity and with a hundred cells, makes this one of the largest madrasas in Morocco. The pitched roofs of the madrasa are covered in part-cylindrical bottle-green glazed ceramic tiles.

**MARINID: CHELLAH, RABAT, MOROCCO** (1310–1339)

Several generations of Marinid sultans are buried in this necropolis. It was damaged by the great Lisbon earthquake of 1755, but it is still possible to grasp the grandeur of what the Marinids built here. The site was occupied first by the Phoenicians or Carthaginians and later by the Romans, who built a walled port city, Sala Colonia, around 40 CE. Marinid Chellah was fortified with huge, crenellated red stone walls and ramparts, ranging from 6 to 20 m (20 to 66 ft) in height. Within these walls now lie untended gardens and Marinid and Roman ruins. It is home to many storks, who have made their nests on the minarets and walls.

OPPOSITE

**SAADIAN TOMBS, MARRAKECH, MOROCCO** (INITIAL CONSTRUCTION 1557; CONSTRUCTION OF 2ND MAUSOLEUM 1603)
The dynastic burial site for the Saadian sultans between 1557 and the first half of the 17th century, the complex consists of two mausolea in a walled garden, accessible through a single narrow corridor. Between the mausolea are large palm trees, orange trees, areas of grass and many flowering shrubs. The interiors show some of the best Moroccan craftsmanship seen anywhere in the country: complex and beautiful geometric compositions in ceramic *zillij* (style of mosaic tilework) combined with very delicate carved plaster (*gebs*). Throughout the gardens are many more tombs (over a hundred graves), mostly marked by rectangular ceramic *zillij* compositions.

RIGHT

**ALAOUITE: BAB AL MANSOUR, MEKNES, MOROCCO** (1732)
Built by Sultan Moulay Ismail, ruler of the Alaouite kingdom for over fifty years, it is a ceremonial gate, the entrance to his imperial city of Meknes – designed to impress. The gate has also served as the location where the city's governor would sit to hear the grievances and disputes of the local population. Its construction marks the symbolic start of the Alaouite dynasty, of which the current Moroccan king is head.

**ALAOUITE: MAUSOLEUM OF MOULAY ISMAIL, MEKNES, MOROCCO** (1703)

Moulay Ismail was the sultan of Morocco from 1672 to 1727, the country's longest-reigning ruler. The site of his mausoleum was chosen in part because it was already the site of the tomb of a 16th-century Moroccan Sufi poet. Constructed by Moulay Ismail in his lifetime, the complex was later added to by his son. The mausoleum is a showcase for Morocco's best craftsmanship in ceramics, painted wood and plaster carving.

**ZAWIYA OF SIDI AHMED AL-TIJANI, FES, MOROCCO** (1782)

The *zawiya*, or religious educational institution, was established by Sheikh al-Tijani, founder of the Tijaniyyah Sufi order. In West Africa, the Sufi order has a strong presence, especially in Senegal. West African pilgrims will often stop off in Fes on their way to Mecca. The façade of the *zawiya* is elaborately ornamented in carved plaster and detailed wooden canopies. It has a square minaret covered in turquoise tiles. The *zawiya* also contains Sheikh al-Tijani's tomb.

**AGHLABID: GREAT MOSQUE OF
KAIROUAN, TUNISIA** (838 CE)

Kairouan is the fourth-holiest city in Islam
(after Mecca, Medina and Jerusalem), and
a mosque existed on this site as early as
670 CE. However, it took on its current
appearance in 856 CE. The minbar is the
oldest dated minbar in Islam and the minaret
the oldest minaret. Its tiered four-sided
shape formed the prototype for minarets in
the western Islamic world. The Blue Quran,
perhaps the most famous calligraphic
manuscript in Islam, was part of the
inventory of the mosque library.

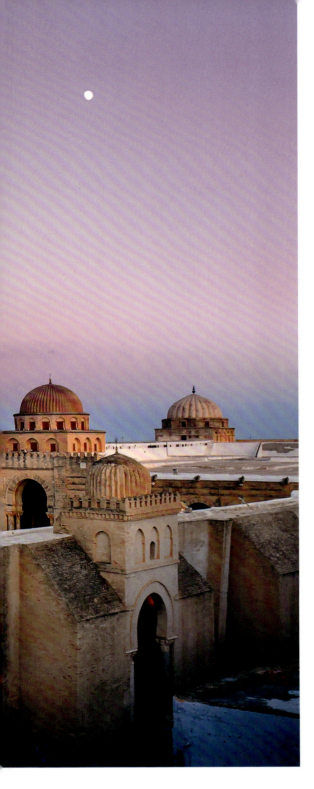

BELOW

## AGHLABID: KALAT EL-KOUBBA FUNDUQ (CARAVANSARAI), SOUSSE, TUNISIA (11TH C)

The notable feature of this caravanserai in the medina (walled old town) of Sousse is its zigzag ribbed dome. Zigzag designs appear across the centuries in Islamic art and architecture. The *kiswah* (cloth) that covers the Kaaba in Mecca has a characteristic zigzag design. The Arabic numerals 7 and 8 form a zigzag when repeated. Depictions of archangels show them with zigzags on their garments. In Islamic architecture, there are domes with vertical or horizontal zigzags. There are minarets with zigzags. As is often the case, there is no historical documentation that can help us understand the motivation behind these design choices.

BELOW

**FADHLOUN MOSQUE, DJERBA, TUNISIA** (11TH C?)

Djerba is known as the island of mosques; it was said it had as many mosques as there are days in a year. The majority belong to the Ibadi community. They served as schools, a refuge in case of attack, places for travellers to stay. The fortified Ibadi mosques on Djerba are small and sober, painted white and without any decoration. Those closer to the coast, like this one, often do not have minarets, but Fadhloun Mosque has a squat minaret that also served as a watchtower. The mosque is said to date from the 11th century, but in there is no mention of it in historical texts.

## AGHLABID: ZAYTUNA MOSQUE, TUNIS, TUNISIA (863 CE)

Many of the columns and stones come from the ruins of nearby Carthage, one of the wealthiest cities of the classical world. It was built at the same time as the Great Mosque of Kairouan (see p. 182), and replaced an earlier mosque. A slave, Fathallah, is mentioned on an inscription on the minaret as overseeing the construction. Over the centuries it has been altered and expanded, but the prayer hall is the same as it was when it was built in the 9th century. Zaytuna Mosque is part of a complex that includes Zaytuna University, one of the world's oldest universities.

## MURADID: SIDI MAHREZ MOSQUE, TUNIS, TUNISIA (1692)

Built in honour of Tunis's patron saint, Sidi Mahrez, by a Muradid bey (governor) of Tunis, the mosque is influenced by the Ottoman architectural design of a central dome surrounded by smaller domes. The interior features Iznik-style ceramic panels on some of the supporting columns. The dome interiors and upper areas of the mosque are covered in delicately carved and pierced plaster, featuring a combination of geometric patterns and vegetal motifs.

**MOZABITE: TOMB AND MAUSOLEUM OF SHEIKH SIDI AÏSSA, MELIKA, ALGERIA** (DATE UNKNOWN)

From the 11th to the 14th century in the M'zab Valley in Algeria, Ibadi Muslims built a network of five oasis towns, known as the M'zab Pentapolis, where they applied strict town planning. They chose to live in isolation and for a thousand years were able to keep their architecture devoid of external influences. Architect Le Corbusier visited in the 1930s, and the simple, functional buildings influenced his modernist masterpiece the Chapel of Ronchamp: plain walls, pure shapes and small apertures.

**MARINID: COMPLEX OF SIDI ABU MADYAN, TLEMCEN, ALGERIA** (1339)

Abu Madyan was a 12th-century Sufi from the area around Seville who settled in Fes, Morocco. His religious and intellectual influence on the western Muslim world has been immense; he is considered one of the most important Sufi masters from the North African tradition. A tomb was constructed for him in Tlemcen, where he died on the way to see the Almohad sultan in Marrakech. The Marinids expanded the tomb complex to what it is now, with a madrasa, baths and a mosque.

**ALMORAVID: GREAT MOSQUE OF TLEMCEN, ALGERIA** (1082)

The mosque was built when the city of Tagrart (present-day Tlemcen) was founded by Emir Yusuf ibn Tashfin. His son was responsible for renovations and embellishment, especially its famed dome, over the *maqsura*, near the mihrab, which has an inscription dating it to 1136. It is made of twelve interlaced arches, built with bricks in line. In between the arches are polygonal plaster panels with curvilinear decorations. At the very top is a round muqarnas composition. The dome is one of the most important examples of Almoravid architecture, and an exceptional masterpiece of Islamic architecture generally.

ABOVE

**HOUARI BOUMEDIENNE VILLAGE, ALGERIA** (1973)

In the 1970s, the Algerian government initiated a programme for the construction of a number of agricultural villages in semi-arid regions as a way to boost the country's agricultural output. Architect Ricardo Bofill took inspiration from the traditional four-iwan courtyard design – a high arched *pishtaq*, flanked by arches – and reduced this to its most essential expression. These courtyards were to be surrounded by dwellings in the tradition of Arab and Mediterranean towns. For a variety of reasons, the project was never completed.

OPPOSITE

**ATIQ MOSQUE, GHADAMES, LIBYA** (1258)

This is the oldest mosque in Ghadames, a Berber oasis town in Libya, dating back to Roman times. It was the most important commercial and cultural centre in the Sahara desert for many centuries; Yemeni traders were the first Arabs to settle here. Adobe is the basic material of construction, along with stone, gypsum, lime and palm trunks. The town seems almost as if it is underground: houses are close together with no windows facing out, and alleyways are covered against the sun. Women are able to visit each other privately by walking across the roofs and covered alleyways.

ABOVE

**GREAT MOSQUE OF AWJILA, LIBYA** (12TH C)

Also known as the Atiq Mosque, this is one of the oldest mosques of North Africa, as well as the oldest in the Sahara. Measuring around 400 m² (4,300 sq ft), it has twenty-one conical domes with small openings to allow ventilation and let in light. Walls are 40 cm (16 in) thick and made of mud brick, limestone and tree trunks. The interior is a maze of worship spaces, created by the columns and arches that support the domes.

OVERLEAF

**GREAT MOSQUE OF DJENNÉ, MALI** (13TH C)

It is the largest free-standing earthen structure in the world. The maintenance of the mud-brick and clay-plaster buildings of Djenné is coordinated by the guild of masons, the Barey Ton. Annual flood waters leave behind a rich mud of mineral deposits, which is mixed into a mortar of cow dung and straw to form the plaster that makes possible huge moulded sculptural façades. Over the centuries, the Great Mosque of Djenné has gone through many changes: expanded, disassembled, demolished, moved, rebuilt. Its current form dates to 1907.

RIGHT

## MOSQUE OF DANI-SARE, DOGON COUNTRY, MALI (DATE UNKNOWN)

Although Islam came to Mali in the 11th century, its reach was mostly limited to urban centres such as Djenné, Dia, Timbuktu and Gao. It was the faith of the ruling elite and trading communities. It was only in the 19th century that it came to remote rural areas such as Dogon country. The mosque in Dani-Sare is built at the centre of the village in the plastered mud-brick style typical of the area.

BELOW

## CENTRAL MOSQUE, YAAMA NIR, TAHOUA REGION, NIGER (1962)

In 1962, the Yamaa village elders decided to build a Friday mosque. Local farmer and occasional builder Falké Barmou was asked to undertake the construction. It resulted in a simple hypostyle mosque made of sun-dried brick and wood. All villagers contributed as they could: some made bricks, some carried bricks, others carried wood and water. Twelve years later the flat roof was replaced with a roof supported by arches with a central dome. The arches were built with bundles of sticks bent and embedded in mud-brick columns. In 1978, four towers were added. The mosque received the 1986 Aga Khan Award for Architecture.

**HIKMA, DANDAJI, NIGER** (2018)

This cultural, educational and religious
complex, which includes a new mosque and
a library (which used to be the old mosque),
was built in a small village in Niger. Designed
collaboratively by Yasaman Esmaili (Studio
Chahar) and Mariam Issoufou Kamara (Atelier
Masōmī), the complex seeks to support,
especially, women and young people to
pursue education. Compressed earth bricks
have been used, as well as other building
materials that could be found in a 5 km
(3 mile) radius of the site.

**KHATMIYA MOSQUE, KASSALA,
SUDAN** (19TH C)

Located near the border with Eritrea, the
mosque is the centre of the Khatmiya
Sufi order, the largest Sufi order in Sudan,
Eritrea and Ethiopia. The large dome tomb
is that of Sayyid Hassan al-Mirghani, son
of the order's founder, Sayyid Muhammad
al-Mirghani al-Khatim, whose lineage goes
back to the Prophet Muhammad. Since the
16th century, Sudan has welcomed men of
religion who spread Islam in remote areas
and were believed to possess the ability to
perform miracles. The introduction of Sufism
occurred through these saintly families, of
whom the Mirghanis were one such.

## ABOVE

### AL-NILIN MOSQUE, OMDURMAN, SUDAN (1984)

'The Mosque of the Two Niles' is located near the confluence of the Blue Nile and the White Nile. It was designed by an architecture student, Qamar al Dawla, who had been asked at short notice to present a design to an architecture exhibition that was to be attended by Sudan's President Nimeiry, who selected the project for construction. Its dome is constructed as a lightweight space-frame covered in an aluminium shell. The interior design theme is Moroccan: carved plaster panels around the arched windows and painted wooden panels with geometric designs on the dome interior.

## LEFT

### BLUE NILE SAILING CLUB STRUCTURE, KHARTOUM, SUDAN (DATE UNKNOWN)

There is a tradition in Islamic societies that land on which a mosque has been built cannot be taken away from the owner. The sailing club members had their eye on a piece of land next to their club, so they built a mini version of the famous al-Nilin Mosque on this land as a way of claiming it. The name of the architect is not known, nor whether it was meant to merely look like a mosque rather than serve as a mosque. It was used for years as a cafeteria.

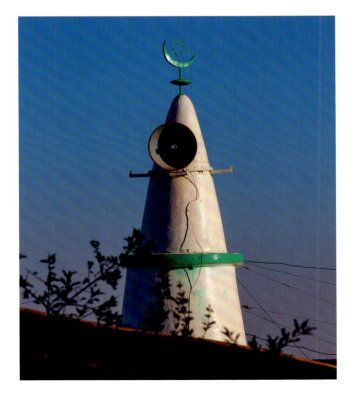

RIGHT

**DIN AGOBARA MOSQUE, HARAR, ETHIOPIA** (DATE UNKNOWN)

Harar is known as the 'city of saints'. It has eighty-two mosques inside the walled city, known as Harar Jugol, which has an area of only about 1 km² (¼ sq mile). Harar was an important centre for trade, connecting Africa, India and the Middle East, and was also a gateway for the spread of Islam in the Horn of Africa. Oral history claims the mosque to have been built 700 years ago, on a rock where the first conversion to Islam took place.

ABOVE

**MOSQUE OF FAKHR AL-DIN, MOGADISHU, SOMALIA** (C. 13TH C)

Named after the first sultan of Mogadishu, the mosque was known for having many finely carved marble decorations, most of which were taken by the sultan of Zanzibar at the end of the 19th century. The marble panel in the mihrab depicts a mosque lamp hanging from a chain, surrounded by floral motifs and calligraphy. Marble is not a locally available stone on the East African coast, and the style and quality of the carving and the creamy-white marble indicate that it was made in Gujarat, India, 3,700 km (2,300 miles) away on the other side of the Arabian Sea. Other marble mihrabs similar in style and material can be found in Tanzania, Kenya and even Iran and Sumatra.

BELOW

**HOUSE OF THE MOSQUE KEEPER, SHELA, LAMU, KENYA** (14TH–15TH C)

A common feature of a traditional Swahili home on the East Coast of Africa is the *zidaka* or *vidaka*: plaster niches in the wall for the display of objects. They can contain books, lamps and other items to indicate the wealth and social standing of the home's occupants. Some of the earliest extant *zidaka* can be found on the island of Lamu, Kenya. A remaining wall of the mosque keeper's house shows elaborate *zidaka* carved in stone.

OPPOSITE

**KIZIMKAZI MOSQUE, DIMBANI, ZANZIBAR, TANZANIA** (1107)

Located on the southern tip of the island of Zanzibar, this may be the oldest Islamic building in East Africa, built by settlers from Shiraz, Iran. Its unusual mihrab, seen here, dates from the 18th century and is said to have been an influence on other Zanzibari mosque architecture.

ABOVE

**OLD FRIDAY MOSQUE, MORONI, COMOROS** (1427)

The Comoro Islands are, like Zanzibar, off the coast of East Africa. Almost the entire population is Muslim; evidence suggests that Islam reached these islands as early as the 8th century. The Old Friday Mosque is the oldest mosque in the capital city of Moroni. A minaret was added in 1921.

OPPOSITE

**MOSQUE OF THE DIVINITY, OUAKAM, DAKAR, SENEGAL** (1997)

A beach with fishing boats separates the mosque from the Atlantic Ocean. In 1973, a local holy man, Muhammad Seyni Guèye, had a dream in which he saw a mosque by the sea. Designed by architect Cheikh Ngom, the mosque has two minarets, 45 m (148 ft) tall, partly covered in green tiles. All the construction was done by the local community.

BELOW

## THE MOSQUES OF BANI, BURKINA FASO (1980s)

In 1979, a mystic in Bani, northern Burkina Faso, had a dream of a mosque. Together with his fellow townspeople, he built this mosque out of wood and the local red clay. When this was finished, they built six other mosques on surrounding hills, all pointing in the direction of the first mosque (so, not with the qiblas in the direction of Mecca). Seen from the sky, the seven mosques are supposed to form the shape of a man with his hands raised in prayer.

BELOW

## MOSQUE, KOUTO, IVORY COAST

(17TH–19TH C)

At one time there were hundreds of Sudanese-style adobe mosques in Ivory Coast, evidence of the influence of the Mali Kingdom to the north and specifically of the famous Great Mosque of Djenné (see pp. 192–93). They have protruding timbers, and the buttresses are crowned with pottery or ostrich eggs, a mixing of local tradition and the Islamic culture that was brought to Ivory Coast through trans-Saharan trade between the 17th and 19th centuries. Now, fewer than two dozen such mosques remain in Ivory Coast.

OVERLEAF

**LARABANGA MOSQUE, LARABANGA, GHANA** (1421)

One of the oldest mosques of West Africa, the Larabanga Mosque is built with timber and packed earth. The mosque has an old Quran, believed to have been received by the founder of the town, Ibrahim Braimah, as a gift from Heaven in answer to his prayers. It is brought out once a year when the start of the new Muslim calendar is celebrated. Muslims and non-Muslims come from all around to hear readings from this Quran, which is thought to reveal insights about the year ahead.

ABOVE

**GREAT MOSQUE OF PORTO-NOVO,
BENIN** (1925)

With its colourful ornamental façade, the
mosque looks more like the type of building
you would find in Portugal, and its two
bell towers might look more at home on
a church. Very different from traditional
West African mosques, it is typical of the
Afro-Brazilian style that was introduced by
the descendants of slaves returning from the
city of Bahia in northeast Brazil. Bahia's 17th-
and 18th-century Baroque churches are the
direct ancestors of this and similar mosques
along the stretch of West African coast
between Lagos, Nigeria, and Porto-Novo in
Benin, from where thousands of slaves were
shipped across the Atlantic.

OPPOSITE

**GOBARAU MOSQUE, KATSINA,
NIGERIA** (1393)

The first Friday mosque in Katsina was built
in 1393 but rebuilt a century later, possibly
under the supervision of Muhammad
al-Maghili, a cleric from Tlemcen, Algeria,
responsible for converting many of the
ruling classes of West Africa to Islam.
Modelled on Sankore Mosque in Timbuktu,
it became a centre of Muslim scholarship
and learning, attracting students and
scholars from across West Africa. Today,
only the 15 m (50 ft)-high minaret remains.

**GIDAN RUMFA, KANO, NIGERIA** (1482)
This is the palace of the emir of Kano. In the 16th century, Kano was the third-largest city in Africa, after Cairo and Fes. The palace was built by, and named after, a famous 15th-century sultan of Kano, Muhammad Rumfa. The largest traditional palace in sub-Saharan Africa, it is set in grounds of more than 13 ha (33 acres) and surrounded by walls 5 m (16 ft) high. Over 1,000 people live and work there. The interiors of the palace are elaborately decorated, with some rooms in red, green and yellow, and others, such as in the photograph, in darker colours. The black is made from a pigment created from the shells of carob seeds. Mica is added to the plaster, giving the walls a silvery sheen. The plaster is burnished with a stone.

# 5
# Asia Pacific

The spread of Islam across the Asia-Pacific region, and the buildings that came with it, is a multifold story that took place over centuries and varies significantly by region and by country. The way Islam and its cultural and religious practices were interpreted and made specific for these regions has had an influence on the architecture. Indonesia, the largest Muslim country in the world, has many such examples. The 18th-century 'underground mosque' in Yogyakarta (see pp. 218–19) combines requirements from Islam and another Javanese religious tradition. The 16th-century Minaret Mosque (see opposite) is one of Indonesia's oldest mosques; the entrance to its grounds is through a *candi bentar*, a special type of stone gate, which looks like an ornamented, stepped structure that has been cleanly cut down the middle and both sides pushed apart to create an entrance. Such elements are typical of the architecture of Java (and Bali), but to most people's minds are not commonly associated with Islamic architecture.

In China there are mosques with pagoda-like wooden minarets, with large projecting ornate rooflines – many of the features associated with traditional Chinese architecture, adapted for Islamic architecture. Such adaptation occurs not just in the features, but also, on occasion, in the plan of a mosque. Xi'an Mosque (see p. 242) is a very large walled compound, with five successive courtyards laid out on a single axis. In this design it borrows from Buddhist temple architecture. China also has the fascinating Apak Khoja Mausoleum in Kashgar, one of the country's most popular tourist destinations, which houses the tombs of several generations of the same family.

**MINARET MOSQUE, KUDUS, JAVA, INDONESIA** (1549)
One of Indonesia's oldest mosques, this used to be called al-Aqsa Mosque. It houses the tomb of Sunan Kudus, one of the Wali Songo, the nine Islamic saints responsible for the spread of Islam on the island of Java. The 20 m (65 ft)-tall minaret is a synthesis of the Hindu-Javanese architectural style and its function in mosque architecture. It is inlaid with blue-and-white ceramic dishes, added in the 19th century. The entrance to the mosque is through a traditional stone split gate (*candi bentar*).

BAYAN BELEQ MOSQUE, LOMBOK,
INDONESIA (17TH C)
Lombok, an island next to Bali, is known as
the Island of a Thousand Mosques. Bayan
Beleq is considered to be the oldest mosque
on Lombok. Built on a stone foundation, it
is made of timber, woven bamboo and palm
thatch. It measures 9 x 9 m (30 x 30 ft) and is
now only used for Islamic festivals.

Apak Khoja came from a line of Sufi teachers, and he and his descendants are credited with bringing Naqshbandi Sufism to China. His granddaughter is the main reason for the large numbers of tourists who come to the mausoleum. Known as the Fragrant Concubine, she is a national legend, immortalized in many plays and texts. A book such as this also presents an opportunity to document the beauty of what has been recently lost, such as Kargilik Mosque in Xinjiang (see p. 217), or what is under threat, such as the Rohingya mosque in Paungdok, Myanmar (see p. 231).

This chapter tells the story of great national mosque projects in postcolonial Muslim-majority countries, including Malaysia, Brunei and Indonesia. The design of these mosques played an important part in the creation of the national identities of these countries. The National Mosque of Malaysia in Kuala Lumpur (see p. 228) is open in its design; you can easily stroll into the grounds and its buildings from the roadside. It was designed as a communal building, accessible to all. Istiqlal Mosque in Jakarta (see p. 220) was opened in 1978, decades after the country's independence; *istiqlal* means 'independence' in Arabic. Brunei now has two national mosques, but before the construction of Sultan Omar Ali Saifuddien Mosque (see p. 236), the capital city had no mosques at all, save for a temporary structure.

It is odd that in a part of the world with such a vast Muslim population, Islamic architecture has been so sparingly documented. Lombok, the Indonesian island next to Bali, is known as the Island of a Thousand Mosques, but it is hard to find much information beyond this phrase. There are thousands of community-built mosques across the Asia-Pacific region, some beautiful in their simplicity, such as the Mubarak Mosque (see p. 224) built by the Cham community in Cambodia. Others are just extraordinary, such as the bright Pink Mosque (see p. 225) in Maguindanao in the Philippines. This chapter cannot do justice to the enormous breadth of diversity of Islamic architecture in this region; it can only show some examples in the hope of conveying some of it.

Moorish Revival architecture swept the globe in the 19th and early 20th centuries, as can be seen in most of the other chapters. This was no different in the Asia-Pacific region. Of special fascination must be the cigar room in a Tokyo palace owned by an influential samurai family (see p. 237). Both floor and ceiling have

OPPOSITE
**KARGILIK MOSQUE, XINJIANG, CHINA**
(1540)
This large old Uyghur mosque, also known as the Friday Mosque of Yecheng, was once elaborately decorated with ceramic compositions on its exterior. It was demolished around 2019 and rebuilt at around a quarter of its size (the entrance gateway, formerly 22 m / 72 ft wide, is now 6 m / 20 ft wide).

OVERLEAF
**SUMUR GUMULING UNDERGROUND MOSQUE, TAMAN SARI COMPLEX, YOGYAKARTA, INDONESIA** (1765)
Part of the Taman Sari Water Palace built during the reign of the first sultan of Yogyakarta, the mosque was a place of prayer but also a place of meditation, following the traditional Javanese religious tradition of Kejawen. The entrance is through an underground corridor that opens into a cylindrical atrium, two storeys high. Four staircases meet in the middle and support a circular platform, from which one more staircase gives access to the top storey. The platform was the location for the sultan's meditation – open to the outside, as Kejawen tradition dictates. In the Sumur Gumuling, the Islamic and Kejawen spiritual requirements of a religious building exist side by side.

geometric star patterns, clearly evoking the Moorish Revival style that was so popular at the time.

The embellishment of buildings is an essential part of Islamic architecture in the Asia-Pacific region as elsewhere. One of the most striking uses of Islamic geometric pattern in contemporary architecture can be found among the railway tracks outside Melbourne's main train station (see p. 238). A simple, angular building that houses a canteen, changing room and other facilities for railway staff seems to have been draped in a complex fivefold geometric composition, the lines of which create irregular window apertures.

It would not have been difficult to fill an entire book with interesting and amazing buildings from the Asia-Pacific region. Quite often they defy our understanding of what is typically Islamic architecture. The region has its own very broad and diverse traditions, sometimes influenced by the most well-known forms in Islamic architecture (tall minaret, central dome, arched entrance iwan and so on), but often more influenced by indigenous design traditions. There is a canonical approach to Islamic architecture in academic research that has excluded the Asia-Pacific region. It means that there is not a single paragraph to be found in the literature on the 16th-century Uyghur Kargilik Mosque (now destroyed), almost any Rohingya mosque in Myanmar (most of them also destroyed) or Cham mosques in Cambodia. Equally, photographs of these significant buildings are also very hard to find. This chapter has tried to capture, in a small way, some of these design traditions and histories. Hopefully, it might spur new research and documentation.

ABOVE

**ISTIQLAL MOSQUE, JAKARTA, INDONESIA** (1978)

This is Indonesia's national mosque, built in commemoration of the country's independence; *istiqlal* means 'independence' in Arabic. The minaret is 6,666 cm (219 ft) in height, in reference to the number of verses in the Quran. The dome over the prayer halls is 45 m (148 ft) in diameter. The mosque was designed by architect Friedrich Silaban, son of a Christian priest in Sumatra.

OPPOSITE

**AL-AQSA MOSQUE, MERAUKE, PAPUA PROVINCE, INDONESIA** (1983)

Located right in the centre of the city of Merauke, the mosque can accommodate 5,000 worshippers. Built over two storeys, it has a very large courtyard. Its central dome and two smaller domes are skilfully covered in glazed tiles with square Kufic calligraphy.

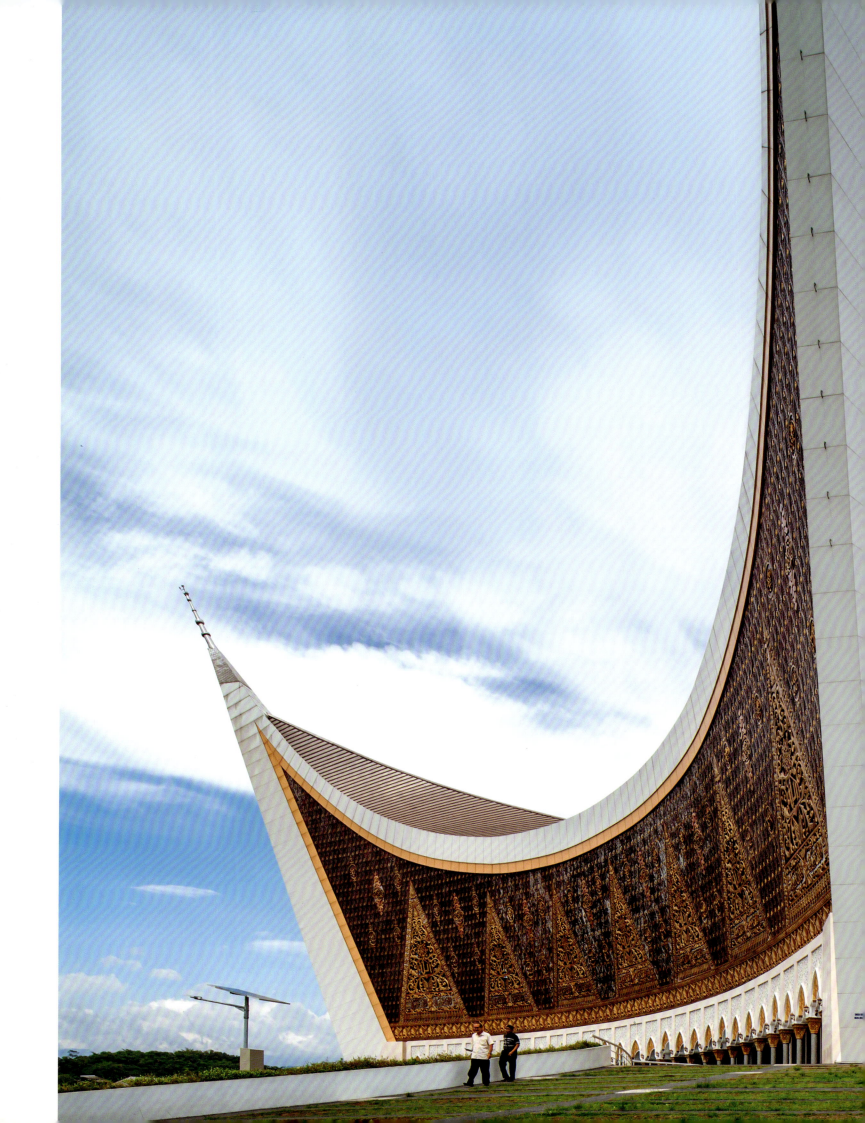

PREVIOUS PAGE
**GRAND MOSQUE OF WEST SUMATRA, PADANG, INDONESIA** (2014)

Its distinctive roof shape was inspired by the traditional spired-roof house of the Minangkabau people. The four corners of the roof curving upwards also reference the Islamic tale of how the young Prophet Muhammad settled a dispute among the Meccan clans on who should carry the Black Stone back to Mecca. He placed the Black Stone in the centre of his unrolled turban, so that it could be carried jointly by the four clan leaders, who each took a corner of the cloth. The pattern on the mosque's exterior references the songket weaving tradition of Sumatra, which combines silk with metallic threads. The mosque was designed by architect Rizal Muslimin.

BELOW
**MUBARAK MOSQUE, PREK PNOV, OUTSIDE PHNOM PENH, CAMBODIA** (LATE 20TH C)

The Cham people are predominantly Muslim; their ancestors moved to Cambodia from what is now Vietnam after the fall of the Champa Empire around 500 years ago. Around 1 per cent of the population of Cambodia is Muslim. Mubarak Mosque, like most mosques in Cambodia, was probably built after the Khmer Rouge era (1975–79). Traditional Cham mosques were often made of wood and had long pitched roofs, but most have disappeared. New Cham mosques are like many new mosques elsewhere in the world, using elements from different Islamic architectural heritages.

**PINK MOSQUE, MAGUINDANAO,
PHILIPPINES** (2014)

Formally named the Dimaukom Mosque
after the mayor and his family who built it,
the mosque was painted pink because it was
their favourite colour, and to represent peace
and love in a part of the Philippines often in
the news for negative reasons. It was built
with the assistance of Christian volunteers.
Many other structures in the town are also
painted pink.

**WHITE MOSQUE BY THE SEA, BONGAO, TAWI-TAWI, PHILIPPINES** (LATE 20TH C?)
Unusually, the front and the back of the mosque are identical. Set in an expanse of green grass and surrounded by a few palm trees, it is the smallest mosque on the island of Tawi-Tawi.

**NATIONAL MOSQUE OF MALAYSIA,
KUALA LUMPUR, MALAYSIA** (1965)
The decision to build a national mosque
for Malaysia was taken very soon after the
country gained independence in 1957. Like
most national mosques built in the 20th
century, it served to help build national
identity. The distinctive roof (now green/
blue but initially pink) was designed to
resemble a parasol, a traditional emblem of
Malay royalty. The large concrete post-and-
beam verandas on stilts reference traditional
Malay domestic architecture. Its architects
were instructed to build a mosque that
would be not just a national monument but
a communal building, open to all Muslims,
rich or poor.

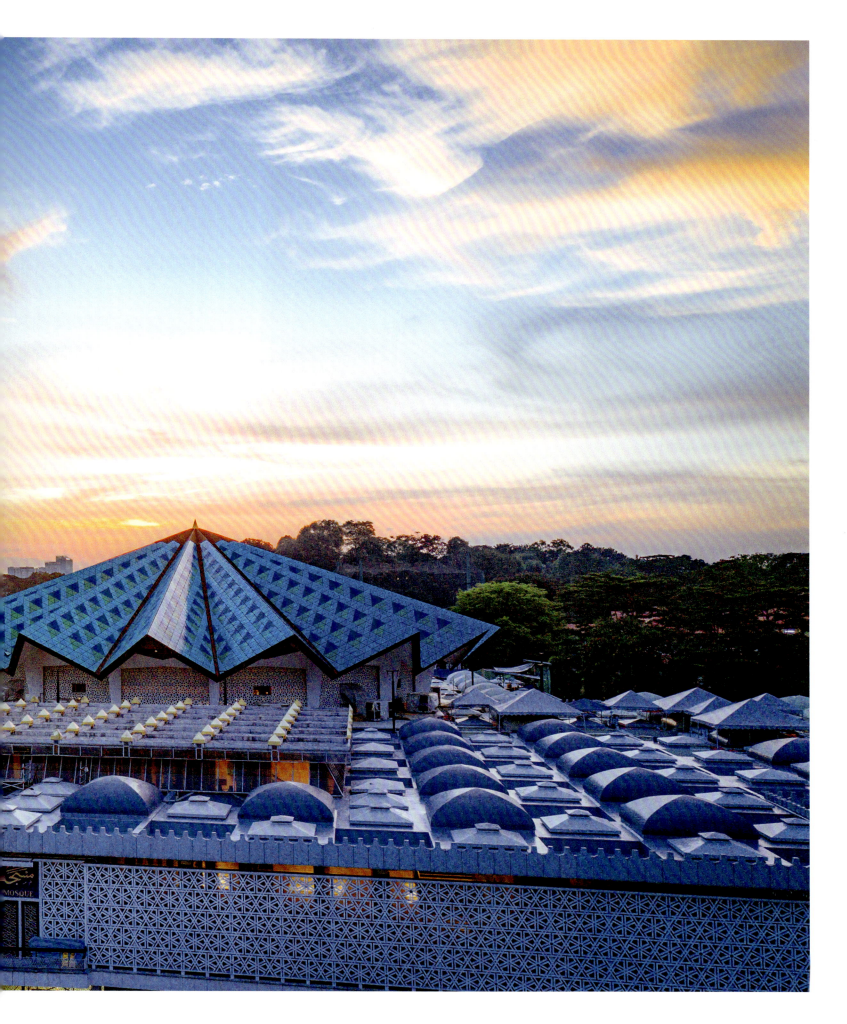

**CRYSTAL MOSQUE, KUALA
TERENGGANU, MALAYSIA** (2008)
The mosque is set in the Islamic Heritage
Park on Wan Man island, which features scale
models of many of the world's most famous
mosques. Made entirely of steel and glass,
it is lit up in the evening with many different
colours alternately radiating through the
glass. When it was built, it was the country's
first 'intelligent mosque', having integrated
IT systems and mosque-wide WiFi with which
visitors can read an electronic Quran.

OPPOSITE, BELOW

**PUTRAJAYA CORPORATION COMPLEX , MALAYSIA** (2004)

The planned city of Putrajaya was built as the new seat of government and Malaysia's administrative and judicial capital. Many of the government buildings are inspired by Islamic architecture; the domes in the background above are part of the Federal Court Building. The large woven-steel archway/*pishtaq* – its pattern inspired by songket weaving (traditional brocade with metallic threads) – is part of the Putrajaya Corporation Complex, and was designed by ZDR Design Consultancy in Malaysia.

ABOVE

**MOSQUE OF PAUNGDOK, RAKHINE STATE, MYANMAR** (DATE UNKNOWN)

Paungdok is a Rohingya village in Rakhine State, Myanmar. Its mosque is thought to be around 500 years old. It is hard to find a mosque in Rakhine State that has not been damaged, destroyed or closed.

**DARUSSALAM MOSQUE, KO PANYI, THAILAND** (DATE UNKNOWN)
This Muslim village in southern Thailand is built on stilts and sheltered by a 200 m (650 ft)-tall limestone rock formation. Established in the late 18th century, the village has expanded over time to include a mosque with gold-coloured domes. About 200 families live in the village.

BELOW

**WADI HUSSEIN MOSQUE, NARATHIWAT, THAILAND** (1634)
The oldest mosque in Thailand, it was built entirely of wood, without the use of nails. Its roof was originally made of sago palm leaves, held together by rattan. In its design it combines local Thai, Chinese and Malay architectural styles.

OPPOSITE

**SULTAN MOSQUE, ROCHOR, SINGAPORE** (1932)
Built on the site of a previous mosque, Sultan Mosque is named after Sultan Tengku Hussein, Raja of Johor, with whose help the East India Company was able to create a trading post in Singapore. Located in the Arab Street neighbourhood, the large golden dome dominates this part of the city, which has been home to Middle Eastern traders since the 19th century. Its design is mostly Mughal in style, although elements from other eras are also found in the building.

LEFT

**SULTAN OMAR ALI SAIFUDDIEN MOSQUE, BANDAR SERI BEGAWAN, BRUNEI** (1958)
Built on an artificial lagoon on the banks of the Brunei River, it is Brunei's national mosque and named after the country's twenty-eighth sultan, who commissioned it and was involved in various aspects of its design. With its golden dome and 52 m (170 ft)-tall minaret, it dominates the skyline of the capital city, Bandar Seri Begawan. It can accommodate 3,000 worshippers.

ABOVE

**OGASAWARA PALACE, TOKYO, JAPAN** (1927)
The palace was built by Count Ogasawara, a member of one of Japan's most influential samurai families. Its cigar room is built in the Moorish Revival style, with a stone-inlay twelvefold geometric star pattern on the floor. The ceiling also has a geometric star design. The exterior of the palace looks like a Spanish colonial building, with a flat roof, tan-coloured stucco walls, elaborate metal window grilles and an ornately carved stone entrance. It is now a restaurant.

**YARDMASTER BUILDING, MELBOURNE, AUSTRALIA** (2009)

Squeezed in amid the railway tracks of Melbourne's Southern Cross station, it is a multi-use facility including offices, break rooms and a gym. Presenting itself to commuters as a jewelry box in the gritty rail environment, it also makes a statement on the value of those who use it. It has a cast-concrete outer shell in which the relief patterns have been polished. The geometric shapes of the fivefold pattern help to create the windows. Seen from the inside, the window shapes are entirely irregular and random; the structure and regularity is all on the outside. The building was designed by McBride Charles Ryan.

**PUNCHBOWL MOSQUE, SYDNEY, AUSTRALIA** (2018)

The mosque is located in the Sydney suburb of Punchbowl, home to a large Lebanese immigrant population. Funded by the community, it was designed by Greek-Australian architect Angelo Candalepas. Built mostly in cast concrete, it accommodates 300 worshippers. The women's gallery is over two balconies, one above the other, that extend into the central prayer space. A central dome is made of concentric layers of wood. The most remarkable features though are the large muqarnas elements. Tiered and angled, they are cast-concrete half-domes, each with a 3 cm (1¼ in) hole through which light streams. The ninety-nine names of Allah are inscribed in the muqarnas units.

**HUAISHENG MOSQUE (MEMORIAL OF THE HOLY PROPHET), GUANGZHOU, CHINA** (1350)

China's first recorded mosque, it is said to have been founded by the Prophet Muhammad's uncle in 627 CE; it has been rebuilt several times. It is also known as the Light Tower Mosque because of its unusual minaret. Standing on a 10 m (33 ft)-high circular stone platform, it is almost 36 m (118 ft) tall. Like most religious buildings in China, it is oriented north–south. An inner monumental gateway bears the inscription 'Religion that holds in great esteem the teachings brought from the Western Region.' Mecca is to the west of China, so the mihrab is on the western wall of the prayer hall.

OPPOSITE

**DA GONGBEI COMPLEX, LINXIA, GANSU PROVINCE, CHINA** (c. 1720)

Built as a mausoleum for Qi Jingyi, who introduced the Qadiriyya Sufi order to China, the complex also has worship space, guest quarters and a visitors' area. 'Gongbei' comes from *gunbad*, the Persian word for dome. It is a term used in northwestern China for a Sufi shrine complex. The city of Linxia has over eighty mosques and more than twenty Sufi shrines. For centuries, it has been one of the main centres of China's Muslim community and is known as China's 'little Mecca'.

**APAK KHOJA MAUSOLEUM COMPLEX, KASHGAR, XINJIANG, CHINA** (1640)

The mausoleum is the resting place of five generations of the Khoja family, a family of religious leaders in large part responsible for bringing Naqshbandi Sufism to Xinjiang. The mausoleum is covered in small glazed tiles, predominantly in greens and blues, showing floral and geometric motifs. Xinjiang's holiest Muslim site, it is visited by thousands of pilgrims every year. The mausoleum is sometimes known as the Tomb of the Fragrant Concubine after Iparhan, granddaughter of Apak Khoja, who, legend has it, so captivated the emperor that he took her to his court in Beijing.

**GREAT MOSQUE OF XI'AN, SHAANXI PROVINCE, CHINA** (1392)

One of China's largest mosques, it covers 12,000 m² (130,000 sq ft). It is thought to have existed since the 7th century CE, though the current mosque dates to the Ming dynasty. It resembles a Buddhist temple, with its single-axis layout along which lie courtyards and pavilions. Three successive courtyards lead to the last one, which contains the prayer hall. Each courtyard contains a central monument, such as a pavilion, screen or tower. In the third courtyard, the Qing Xiu Dian (Place of Meditation), is the octagonal Tower of the Visiting Heart, the tallest structure of the complex. Nowadays most visitors to the mosque are tourists rather than pilgrims.

# 6

# Europe & the Americas

The story of Islamic architecture in this chapter is mostly a story of influence and inspiration: the influence of the Great Mosque of Córdoba (see opposite) on Islamic Architecture in the western Mediterranean generally; the influence of western Mediterranean Islamic architecture on the architecture of Europe, as can be seen in, for example, Amalfi Cathedral (see p. 274) and the Doge's Palace and St Mark's Basilica in Venice (see pp. 274–75). It is also the story of the transfer of ideas and visual traditions from one region to another, one society to another and one societal group to another.

There has been such an interchange of ideas and influences between Islamic and non-Islamic cultures that using the label 'Islamic architecture' can actually be more of a hindrance to understanding than a help. Consider the twenty or so 10th-century Serrablo churches in the north of Spain (see p. 261). Most of Spain was under Umayyad rule from their capital in Córdoba. Some Christian kingdoms in the north held on and grew in population thanks to the influx of Christians from the south. The Serrablo churches were built in a short period of time and are all similar in size and design. They have horseshoe-arched windows and slender belltowers that look like minarets. Even though we now associate the horseshoe arch very much with Islamic architecture, for the Christians who left southern Spain and built churches in their new home in the north, there might not have been such a strong association; it seems to have been no more than an architectural feature that either was considered appropriate for houses of worship generally or was used only for its visual appeal. Consider also the

**UMAYYADS IN SPAIN: GREAT MOSQUE OF CÓRDOBA, SPAIN** (EST. 786 CE)
The prayer hall presents itself as an infinite forest of columns and arches. The double arches raise the height of the hall, their alternating red and white voussoirs (wedge-shaped elements) making reference to the Dome of the Rock (see pp. 12 and 47) and the Umayyad Mosque in Damascus (see pp. 10 and 40), monumental masterpieces with which the Umayyads in Spain wanted to show their ancestral connection. See also pp. 250–52.

Thanks-Giving Chapel from 1976 in Dallas, Texas (see p. 304), whose spiral design brings to mind the Abbasid minarets of Abu Dulaf Mosque and the Great Mosque of Samarra, both in Iraq. What the northern Spanish churches and the chapel in Dallas share is that the indebtedness to Islamic architecture is evident even though we often do not have insight into the motives of the designers. Also in the USA is Marin County Civic Center by Frank Lloyd Wright (see p. 303). The huge, wide dome and the countless arches along the exterior, together with the very slender tower, combine the most distinctive elements of Islamic architecture. In the case of Wright, we do know that at the time of the design of this project, he was also working on a large design project in Baghdad (never built).

When we think of Islamic architecture in Europe, the Alhambra in Granada (see pp. 256–59) or the Great Mosque of Córdoba are probably the first to come to mind. Both are extremely interesting and beautiful; entire careers have been dedicated to studying them, so it is hard to present such buildings in a concise way. The architectural features of the Great Mosque of Córdoba greatly influenced mosque design, but in architecture it is sometimes also interesting to look at the plan of a building, not just the interior and exterior. Córdoba shows that the many extensions of the mosque were done with simple geometry – drawing circles and extending lines. It makes it easy to imagine these builders planning their extensions, letting the obvious and elegant dimensions of geometry present them with choices.

The Church of Santo Domingo in Quito, Ecuador (see p. 310), has an exceptionally fine coffered ceiling with interlacing wooden patterns, much like you can find in Spain and Portugal. When Spain started to exploit this part of the world, only Spanish Christians were encouraged to emigrate. Muslims living in Spain (known as Mudejars) emigrated secretly to South America, usually as stowaways, and Mudejar craftsmen introduced the architectural traditions from Andalusia to this part of the world. There are dozens of Mudejar buildings and features in Central and South America. The kiosk of Chignahuapan in Puebla, Mexico (see opposite), is similarly indebted to the skills of these Mudejar migrants.

Examples of 19th- and early 20th-century interpretations of Islamic architecture could fill an entire book – from the exaggerated ceramic-glazed horseshoe-arched entrance of the public baths in

**MUDEJAR KIOSK OF CHIGNAHUAPAN, PUEBLA, MEXICO** (EARLY 20TH C)
Mudejar art was typically seen in Latin America as a product of the triumph of the Christian Reconquest in Spain. It was also seen as the quintessential Spanish national style. Lastly, the defeat of Granada (the last Muslim enclave in Spain) and the 'discovery of the Americas', both Spanish achievements, occurred in 1492, mythically and historically linking the events together. All these factors influenced the design of, for example, this wooden kiosk. Richly decorated with painted patterns and painted versions of plaster designs of al-Andalus and North Africa, it also features indigenous Mexican patterns. Under the kiosk platform is a water fountain.

Dunkirk (see p. 284), France, to the *bismillah* around the entrance to what was once Bloomingdale's department store in Chicago (see p. 304). It was fashionable for 19th-century European aristocrats to build palaces with features that borrowed from Islamic, especially Moorish, architecture: a Russian prince built his 'Crimean Alhambra' (see p. 283); King Ludwig II of Bavaria had a 'Moorish kiosk' erected in the grounds of his Schloss Linderhof (see p. 290). Successful 19th-century authors spent money on creating imaginative interiors inspired by 'the East'. French author Pierre Loti created a Turkish salon, an Arab salon and a mosque in his childhood home. Alexander Dumas' home, the Château de Monte-Cristo, had a Moorish room. Even Napoleon III and Empress Eugénie had an imperial chapel built, decorated with geometric patterns and tiles from Morocco.

Thousands of mosques can be found across Europe and the Americas, most of them built relatively recently. Many of them take their explicit inspiration from the heritage of Islamic architecture, especially from the Ottoman era, and from North African design elements. Many of them try to find a balance between heritage and their European or American environment.

## UMAYYADS IN SPAIN: GREAT MOSQUE OF CÓRDOBA, SPAIN (EST. 786 CE)

Under Caliph Abd al-Rahman, the mosque in Córdoba became the ultimate expression of the Umayyads' perceived place in the world and their commitment to science and art. After the fall of the caliphate, the mosque was neglected, until in 1162 the Almohads declared Córdoba their capital in al-Andalus and renovations were carried out. In 1236, as a result of the Reconquista (Christian Reconquest), the mosque was converted to a Roman Catholic cathedral, dedicated to the Virgin Mary. In the 16th century, a large cathedral structure was built in the middle of the mosque. Even at the time, this was controversial.

## UMAYYADS IN SPAIN: BAPTISTERY GATE, GREAT MOSQUE OF CÓRDOBA, SPAIN (EST. 786 CE)

This gate is located on the eastern side and was built as part of the mosque extension of al-Mansur towards the end of the 10th century. It is thought that the expansion, which almost doubled the mosque in size, was necessary owing to the influx of Berbers from North Africa. The Great Mosque of Córdoba has around twenty exterior doorways from different eras. Many are elaborately decorated with arches, plaster and brick compositions.

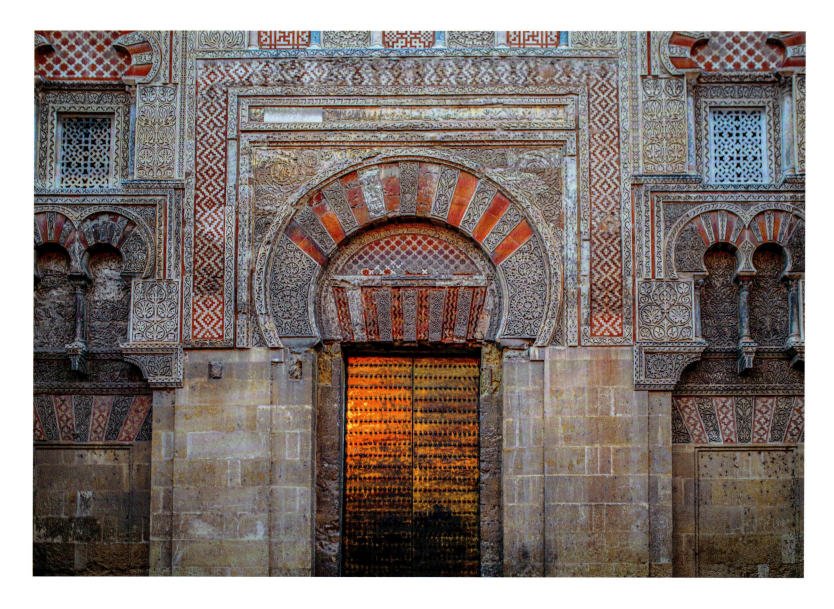

### UMAYYADS IN SPAIN: CARVED STONE WINDOW, GREAT MOSQUE OF CÓRDOBA, SPAIN (EST. 786 CE)

The unique and innovative fourfold composition shows the imagination and skill of the craftsman. It has only three different shapes: a big square, a small square (rotated) and a five-sided shape.

### UMAYYADS IN SPAIN: SALÓN RICO, MADINAT AL-ZAHRA, CÓRDOBA, SPAIN (EST. 936 CE)

The Salón Rico is the most splendid interior space in the palace-city of Madinat al-Zahra. It was built for the use of Caliph Abd al-Rahman III. It is a large hall of 20 x 17.5 m (66 x 57 ft) with large openings to the front, looking out over a terraced garden and the Guadalquivir valley. The interior features many carved marble and limestone panels, depicting vegetation. It is documented that the caliph's eunuch Sunaif was in charge of the exquisite decoration.

### UMAYYADS IN SPAIN: GORMAZ CASTLE, CASTILE AND LEON, SPAIN (965 CE)

The hill, on which a fortress has existed since before the Umayyads came to Spain, was a natural bridgehead on the border between Muslim and Christian lands and as such the castle changed hands frequently over the centuries. It was seized in 965 CE during the reign of al-Hakam II to defend the borders of the Caliphate of Córdoba. Most of the defensive features date from this period. Europe's largest castle for centuries, it measures 380 x 63 m (1,250 x 206 ft) at its widest point and has twenty-seven towers. As was typical of fortress architecture at the time, the towers were connected to the walls only at their base so that in case of attack, a tower might be destroyed but the wall would remain standing.

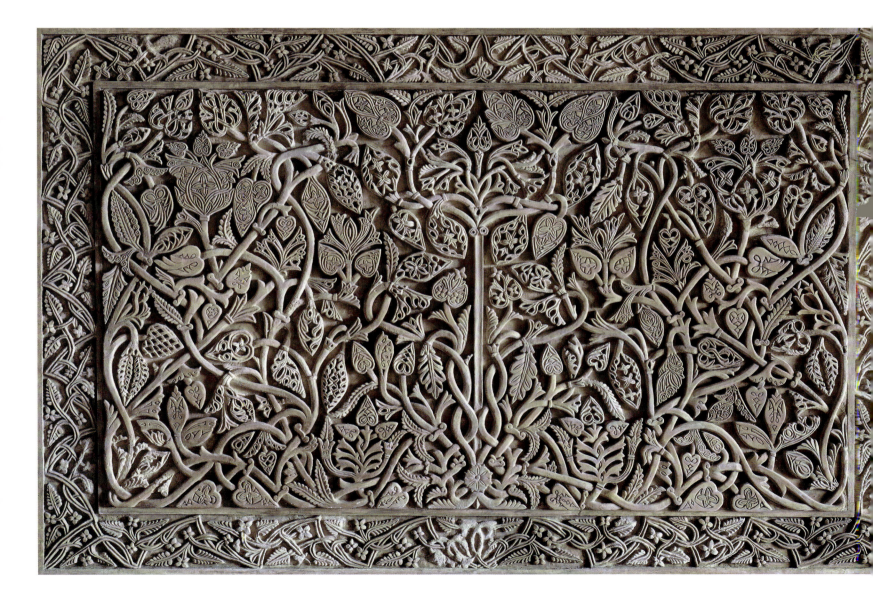

**NASRID: ALHAMBRA, GRANADA, SPAIN** (EST. 1238)

The Alhambra was founded by the Nasrids and formed a city-citadel, separate from Granada below. The Nasrid palaces in the citadel are mostly on the northern side (visible in the photograph), overlooking Granada's Albaicín quarter. They are designed as was common in North African architecture, featuring a courtyard with a pool or fountain in its centre and rooms and halls arranged around it. The view of the Alhambra seen here was taken from the famous Mirador de San Nicolas.

BELOW

**NASRID: PALACE OF THE LIONS, ALHAMBRA, GRANADA, SPAIN** (EST. 1238)

The Palace of the Lions has a courtyard measuring 35 x 24 m (115 x 79 ft). The famous fountain in the centre consists of a twelve-sided marble basin supported by twelve stone lions. Water streams through four channels, representing the four rivers of Paradise, dividing the courtyard into four. The channels lead to four separate spaces. On the basin is a poem by Ibn Zamrak, which includes the following lines:

*For, are there not in this garden wonders
that God has made incomparable
in their beauty,
and a sculpture of pearls with
a transparent light,
whose borders are trimmed with seed pearls?
Melted silver flows through the pearls,
which it resembles in its pure dawn beauty.
Water and marble seem to be one,
without letting us know which of
them is flowing.
Don't you see how the water spills
on the basin,
but its spouts hide it immediately?
It is a lover whose eyelids are brimming
over with tears,
tears that it hides from fear of a betrayer.*

**NASRID: HALL OF THE ABENCERRAJES,
ALHAMBRA, GRANADA, SPAIN**
(1377–1390)

The Hall of the Abencerrajes is part of the
Palace of the Lions, considered to be the
most awe-inspiring and beautiful part of the
Alhambra. The dome over the hall is shaped
by thousands of plaster muqarnas elements,
working together to create a delicate and
dense three-dimensional composition that
seems to defy gravity and almost touch
infinity. The Palace of the Lions is graced
with two extraordinary plaster muqarnas
dome interiors: this one, which is shaped like
an eight-pointed star, and the other in the
Hall of the Two Sisters, which is shaped like
an octagon.

**NASRID: MIRADOR DE LINDARAJA,
HALL OF THE TWO SISTERS, ALHAMBRA,
GRANADA, SPAIN** (1354–1358)

During the Nasrid era, beyond the arches
was the countryside, and the mirador
served as a watchtower. Now it looks out
over the Daraxa Gardens. The geometric
compositions in the mirador, made from cut
tile (*zillij*), are some of the finest in all of the
Nasrid palaces in the Alhambra. The same
goes for the carved stucco above the arches.
The name 'Lindaraja' comes from the Arabic
*Ayn Dar Aisha* ('the eyes of Aisha's house').

LEFT

**MOZARAB: CHURCH OF SANTA EULALIA DE SUSÍN, ARAGON, SPAIN** (950–1024)

In the north of Spain, in the foothills of the Pyrenees, is a group of around twenty small churches, known as the Serrablo churches built by Christians who remained after the Umayyad conquest. They are similar in size, shape and features, with a narrow nave, an apse and a slim belltower that resembles a minaret. They combine Romanesque features with Mozarabic features such as windows with horseshoe arches set in an *alfiz* (rectangular frame). After the Reconquista, the population was encouraged to leave the mountainous region and the villages became depopulated, meaning that these churches have changed little over the centuries.

BELOW

**MUDEJAR: HERMITAGE OF OUR LADY OF THE FOUNTAINS, AMUSCO, SPAIN** (MID-13TH C)

The hermitage was built during the transition from Romanesque to Gothic architecture, as can be seen in its mixture of semicircular and more pointed arches. Its pulpit, seen below, is a masterpiece of Mudejar stone carving. The banister panel has a fourfold pattern of interlacing indented square shapes.

OPPOSITE

**MOZARAB: HERMITAGE OF SAN BAUDELIO DE BERLANGA, CALTOJAR, SPAIN** (EARLY 11TH C)

Set in a remote location among rolling hills, this hermitage church is plain on the outside, but its interior is a marvel of Mozarabic architecture. Almost all its surfaces are painted, and in the centre of the main space is a column from which eight slight horseshoe arches spring. It looks like a palm tree, one of the symbols of Saint Baudelius, to whom the building is dedicated. The walls are painted in the secco technique (painting on dry plaster), depicting scenes from the Bible, and hunting scenes and animals derived from Islamic art. Many of the ornamental elements show their indebtedness to Islamic visual motifs. A majority of the wall paintings were removed in the early 20th century and can now be found in several major museums.

LEFT

### MUDEJAR: REAL ALCÁZAR, SEVILLE, SPAIN (1366)

Nothing remains of the original 10th-century Islamic fortress-palace; the most significant additions and renovations were done by Mudejar craftsmen under two different Christian kings in the 14th century. Alfonso XI of Castile sought to claim Islamic visual culture in the same way that he had claimed Islamic territory in his victory over the Nasrids and Marinids in 1340. King Pedro (son of Alfonso), on the other hand, had grown up in Seville, surrounded by Islamic art. He was advised by exiled Nasrid sultan Muhammad V of Granada. This explains to a large extent why the Alcazar resembles the Alhambra so much (see pp. 256–59).

BELOW

### MUDEJAR: CATHEDRAL OF THE SAVIOUR, ZARAGOZA, SPAIN (1318)

In 1318 the archbishopric of Zaragoza was created and a new Gothic church built. A chapel, La Parroquieta, was added, whose exterior is now considered a masterpiece of Mudejar brickwork. Pope Benedict XIII (who ruled from Avignon, not Rome, and as such is a historical 'antipope'), was heavily involved in other modifications and improvements to the cathedral. The Almohad-style battlements on top of the Mudejar elevations make that part of the cathedral almost look like a castle. The pope had a fondness for Mudejar architecture, as can be seen in the large number of buildings he commissioned in the Aragon region.

**MUDEJAR: CHURCH OF SAN ROMÁN, TOLEDO, SPAIN** (13TH C)

The interior is a synthesis of the different styles and influences that were present in Toledo in the 13th century: Mozarabic horseshoe and polylobed arches, rectangular *alfiz* frames around some of the arches and geometric patterns. On the insides of the arches are Byzantine-style paintings of winged angels and saints. Above the arches are windows framed by pseudo-Arabic calligraphy and Latin inscriptions. The wall painting shows the scene described in Matthew 27:52, where the saints rose from their tombs at the moment that Jesus Christ died on the Cross.

**MUDEJAR: SYNAGOGUE SANTA MARIA LA BLANCA, TOLEDO, SPAIN** (1205)

Originally known as the Synagogue of Ibn Shushan, it is one of the oldest synagogues in Europe. Ibn Shushan was finance minister for Alfonso VIII of Castile and is recorded as patron of this synagogue (or perhaps of its restoration). Toledo was well known for the harmonious coexistence of Muslims, Jews and Christians in an era known as La Convivencia. The decoration of the capitals atop the columns with ornamental pinecones shows the influence of Almohad architectural decoration.

LEFT

### MONASTERY OF SAN JUAN DE DUERO, SORIA, SPAIN (13TH C)

The monastery was built by the Order of Knights of the Hospital of Saint John of Jerusalem. The unique combination of different arch types (pointed arches, intersecting arches, pointed horseshoe arches) that reference Islamic architecture in the cloisters has led many to conclude that its design involved Mudejar architects and masons. There is a small church that predates the cloisters to which the Knights added two small shrines inside (aedicules) that also distinctly show the influence of Mudejar architectural knowledge. It was abandoned in the mid-18th century.

RIGHT

### ARCHITECTURAL MAQUETTE, SPAIN (LATE 19TH C)

A three-dimensional model of the Bayt al-Maslaj, or Bed Room, part of the hammam in the Comares Palace, the most important palace of the Alhambra: the sultan's official residence. The wooden maquette in a cabinet was made in the workshop of sculptor Diego Fernández Castro in Granada. Low-relief models were much more common. The amount of accurate detail in this three-dimensional maquette probably means that a craftsman was involved who had worked on the restoration of this part of the Alhambra. There was demand in Europe in the 19th century for high-quality souvenirs from famous destinations.

OPPOSITE

### MUDEJAR: ROYAL MONASTERY OF SANTA MARÍA DE GUADALUPE, EXTREMADURA, SPAIN (14TH C)

One of Spain's most important monasteries, it originated as a chapel built in the late 13th century. After King Alfonso XI's victory against the Marinids in 1340, he declared the chapel a royal sanctuary. The Roman Catholic kings made a pilgrimage to the monastery after their reconquest of Granada in 1492, the same year as the 'discovery' of the Americas. In 1496 Christopher Columbus visited the monastery, bringing two Mexicans to be baptized. Santa María of Guadalupe was made patron of Spain's territories in the New World. The two-storey cloisters of the monastery are built in Mudejar style. An astounding rose window combines traditional Gothic elements with a twelvefold Islamic geometric star pattern.

ABOVE

**CASA VICENS, BARCELONA, SPAIN** (1883)
Designed by Antoni Gaudí, this was his first significant commission after graduating from architecture school five years earlier. Both interior and exterior showcase Gaudí's unbridled creative genius. It mixes up many architectural traditions from Spain, especially Islamic architecture. It also has Art Nouveau influences and is considered one of Spain's first modernist masterpieces. It has Moorish arches and tiling patterns on the outside, and a muqarnas composition inside.

OPPOSITE

**GRAND MOSQUE OF GRANADA, SPAIN** (2003)
It is the first mosque to be built in Granada since the Reconquista of 1492. Located in Albaicín, the old Arab quarter, the mosque has a public garden that offers a breathtaking view of the Alhambra on the opposite hill (similar to the view on pp. 256–57). Architect Sidi Karim Viudes designed a magnificent and innovative cubic muqarnas composition made of plastered wood in the entrance hall. The facets of the muqarnas (7 x 7 cm / 2¾ x 2¾ in) were painted by artist Daud Al Mursi. The location and features of the mosque are focused on accessibility, especially towards non-Muslims, an issue close to the hearts of the Muslim convert community that built the mosque.

RIGHT
**PALACE CHAPEL, SINTRA, PORTUGAL** (c. 14th c)
Sintra Palace near Lisbon is located on the site of a castle built by the Moorish rulers of Lisbon. Nothing from that period survives, and the chapel is now the oldest part of the palace, which was mainly built during the 15th and 16th centuries. The Mudejar ceiling of the chapel is one of the best preserved in Portugal. The wall paintings depict doves (restored in the 20th century), symbolizing the Holy Ghost.

LEFT
**MOZARAB: CHURCH OF SÃO PEDRO, LOUROSA, PORTUGAL** (912 CE)
This small basilica is considered to be the most significant Mozarab building in Portugal. The central nave is separated from two side naves by horseshoe arches on columns. There are several other details that show the influence of Andalusian architecture.

**ABOVE & RIGHT**

## NORMAN SICILY: ZISA PALACE, PALERMO, ITALY (1189)

Set in a luxuriant garden park, the palace-castle was built by Arab craftsmen and builders in the Fatimid style. A rectangular pool in front of the building cools the warm air before it enters the Fountain Hall (above). The Fountain Hall is clad in marble; water flows from a fountain in the far wall down a corrugated marble slope into a succession of small canals and basins in the floor, which connect to the pool outside through an underground passage. Above the fountain is a mosaic depicting peacocks, archers and date palms. Above that is a complex muqarnas composition carved from local sandstone. Throughout the Zisa Palace there are mosaics depicting flora and hunting scenes, showing both Byzantine and Islamic influences.

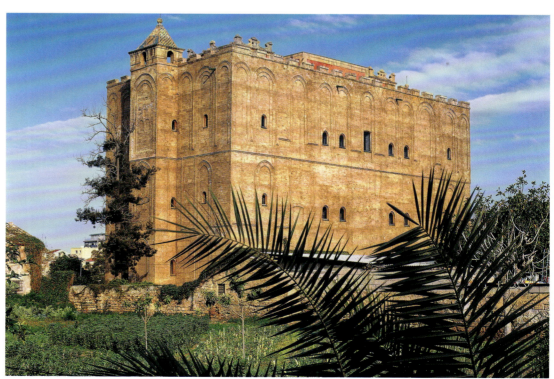

**ABOVE & RIGHT**
**NORMAN SICILY: PALATINE CHAPEL,
PALERMO, ITALY** (1140)
Construction started at the behest of Roger
II, Norman king of Sicily and Africa, and work
was continued by his successors. The walls
and arches are covered in mosaics in the
Byzantine style. The central ceiling is covered
in wooden muqarnas, arranged in two rows
of eight-pointed stars. The surfaces of the
muqarnas are painted in immense detail,
depicting human figures, animals, plants,
leaves and tendrils.

**OPPOSITE**
**CHURCH OF SANTA MARIA
DELL'AMMIRAGLIO, PALERMO,
ITALY** (1143)
The founder of the church, George of
Antioch, was a commander in the navy of
Roger II of Sicily. The interior has some
of the finest gold mosaics in Sicily, showing
Roger II receiving a crown from Christ (not
from the Pope, significantly). There is a Kufic
Arabic inscription on a marble column that
has the *bismillah*. Around the dome is a
frieze in which a Christian hymn has been
written in Arabic. The bell tower was added
somewhat later and features a very wide
range of details, many of them from
Islamic architecture.

ABOVE

### CATHEDRAL OF ST ANDREW, AMALFI, ITALY (13TH C)

For a while Amalfi was the most important commercial centre in the western Mediterranean. The cathedral was built to house the relics of the apostle Andrew, which were brought to Amalfi after the Sack of Constantinople in 1204. The cathedral's black and white ('ablaq') exterior and its pointed arches are imports from Syria.

RIGHT

### ST MARK'S BASILICA (BEGUN 1063) AND DOGE'S PALACE, VENICE, ITALY (BEGUN 1340)

Between 1100 and 1500 Venice was at its peak, at the centre of trade between East and West, and a station on the pilgrimage route to Jerusalem. Venetians adopted aspects of the architecture they saw in other great trading cities such as Cairo, Alexandria, Damascus and Aleppo. St Mark's Basilica expresses the power and magnificence of Venice more than any other building in the city. The high domes were made possible by the adoption of the double dome construction (an interior dome and a taller exterior dome). The Doge's Palace is thought to have been inadvertently modelled on al-Aqsa Mosque (see p. 47), which at the time was mistaken for Solomon's Palace. Its white Istrian stone and red Verona marble façade with lozenge designs is reminiscent of brickwork patterns from Anatolia and Iran. Its most distinctive feature though is probably the façade-wide row of thirty-four ogee (teardrop-shaped) arches, which first made an appearance on the Great Minaret of Aleppo (see p. 41).

OVERLEAF
**CASTELLO DI SAMMEZZANO, LECCIO, ITALY** (c. 1605; 1840s–1889)
Originally built in the early 17th century, it was remodelled in the 19th century by Ferdinando Panciatichi Ximenes, taking inspiration from, and interpreting, Islamic architecture. There are visual elements from the Alhambra, the Taj Mahal, the Alcazar, Persian architecture and Cairo mosque architecture. He started in the late 1840s and it became his lifelong project. After his death, his daughter ensured that his vision was completed. The palazzo has 365 rooms, each of which is decorated in a different style.

**MOSQUE OF ROME, ITALY** (1995)

It occupies a plot of 30,000 m² (323,000 sq ft) that also includes a library building and cultural centre. It is one of the largest mosque complexes in Europe. Clad in pale red bricks, combined with brown travertine and green peperino stone, it references local Roman building traditions. The prayer hall is 40 x 40 m (130 x 130 ft) and has thirty-two columns that consist of four shafts tapering slightly before opening up towards the top, suggesting the form of hands opened in prayer. The architects were Paolo Portoghesi, Vittorio Gigliotti and Sami Mousawi.

**ABOVE**

**QASIM KHANATE: KHAN'S MOSQUE, KASIMOV, RUSSIA** (MID-16TH C; 2ND HALF 18TH C)

Kasimov was the capital of the Qasim Khanate from 1452 to 1681. The minaret is all that remains of the original mosque, most of which was demolished by Peter the Great in 1702. In 1773, Catherine the Great issued the Toleration of All Faiths edict, and the mosque in Kasimov was revived and rebuilt. Its fortunes over the centuries have risen and fallen with the societal and political upheavals in Russia generally.

**RIGHT**

**ST PETERSBURG MOSQUE, RUSSIA** (1921)

The mosque is modelled on the Gur Amir (Timur's tomb) in Samarkand, a city that was considered a spiritual centre in the pre-Revolutionary Russian Empire. Much of the exterior of the mosque is clad in black granite. The most distinctive aspect is its ribbed dome (like the Gur Amir's), its entrance portal and the women's entrance at the side: all are covered in predominantly blue and turquoise ceramic tiles from the workshop of Peter Kuzmich Vaulin (who reintroduced majolica to Russia).

### TAUBA MOSQUE, NABEREZHNYE CHELNY, TATARSTAN, RUSSIA (1992)

It is a modern, angular building that perhaps looks more like a church than a mosque. It was completed just after the collapse of the Soviet Union, when Tatarstan became subject to a great deal of interest from Muslim countries and educational institutions. Its exterior walls are covered in grey limestone and the roof is copper. The mosque initially incorporated stained-glass windows that also included crosses and Stars of David, as per the wishes of the USSR era's most senior Muslim faith leader.

### MUKHTAROV MOSQUE, VLADIKAVKAZ, RUSSIA (1908)

The mosque was built by Polish architect Józef Płośko, who took his inspiration from the architecture of Cairo, especially al-Azhar Mosque (see pp. 29 and 32). The wish for a mosque in the city was first expressed by Tatar soldiers in 1863. Over the next decades efforts were made to get permission and to raise funds; the mosque is named after Azerbaijani oil tycoon Murtuza Mukhtarov, who stepped in to finance its construction. The interior is extraordinarily colourful, exuberant and idiosyncratic in its design.

**SPANISH SYNAGOGUE, PRAGUE, CZECH REPUBLIC** (1868)

Built to replace what was probably the oldest synagogue in Prague, it is in the Moorish Revival style. The extraordinary interior was designed by Antonín Baum and Bedřich Münzberger. In the second half of the 19th century, hundreds of synagogues around the world were built in the Moorish Revival style. Interestingly, these did not serve the Sephardic Jewish communities (who were exiled from Spain in 1492) but instead served the Ashkenazi Jewish communities from Eastern and Central Europe, for whom this style referenced a time when Jews were part of mainstream society in medieval al-Andalus.

**VORONTSOV PALACE, CRIMEA, UKRAINE** (1837)

Built by British architect Edward Blore, this was sometimes referred to as the Crimean Alhambra. It is a hybrid of Moorish Revival, Neo-Mughal and Gothic Revival architectural elements and ornamentation. Russian aristocrats, including Tsar Nicolas I, visited Vorontosv Palace, and were motivated to build their own summer palaces in a similar style in Crimea. Tsar Nicholas I even had a bathroom for his wife designed in his Winter Palace in St Petersburg in the style of the Alhambra. The empress's new bathroom was instrumental in the further spread of the Moorish Revival style in Russia. It was designed by Russian architect Aleksandr Briullov, who was almost singlehandedly responsible for Russia's Moorish Revival architecture.

BAINS DUNKERQUOIS

LEFT

**DUNKIRK BATHS BUILDING, DUNKIRK, FRANCE** (1897)

To improve the health of the citizens of 19th-century Dunkirk, the local mayor authorized several public projects to improve hygiene conditions for the city's inhabitants. The public baths of Dunkirk were one such project. Lille architects Albert Baert, Louis Gilquin and Georges Boidin proposed a Moorish Revival building. It offered the local population showers, a public laundry and a swimming pool. The large chimney, which had the appearance of a minaret, and two columns capped with small onion domes and a half moon have since disappeared.

ABOVE

**MISSIRI, FRÉJUS, FRANCE** (1930)

Built by the French army to boost the morale of the Senegalese colonial troops, the Tirailleurs, the Missiri ('mosque' in the West African Bambara language) was styled on the Great Mosque of Djenné (see p. 191), though it served as a community centre and never had a religious purpose. It has no qibla wall, no mihrab and no covered prayer area. For the African colonial soldiers stationed in Fréjus, or passing through on their way to war, the Missiri was a solemn presence. African soldiers killed in battle were carried through and around the Missiri and prayers were held in an open area (*musalla*) outside the building. Around the building, the French army built fake termite mounds of poured concrete and painted them red to enhance the West African feel of the Missiri.

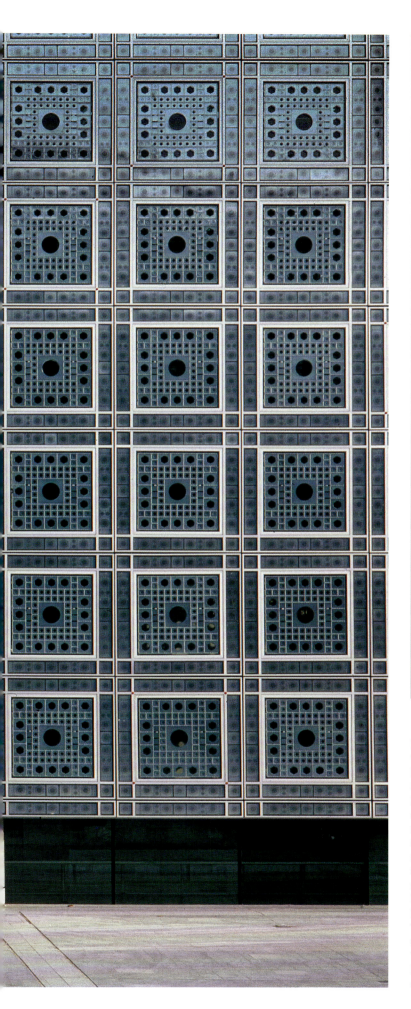

### INSTITUT DU MONDE ARABE (ARAB WORLD INSTITUTE), PARIS, FRANCE (1987)

Its prominent location on the Left Bank in the centre of Paris is meant to serve as an illustration of the dialogue between Western culture and the Arab world. The exterior is covered by a metal structure of rationally arranged big and small squares, reminiscent of geometric composition. Inside these squares are electromechanical mechanisms (like camera diaphragms) that moderate how much daylight enters the building. The brighter it is outside, the more they close. There are around 3,000 large and small diaphragm mechanisms on the façade. The building was designed by Jean Nouvel, Pierre Soria and Gilbert Lézénès, with the Architecture Studio.

**GREAT TRANSEPT, CLUNY ABBEY, BURGUNDY, FRANCE** (1120)

Built between 1088 and 1120, the church was the third on the site, and is commonly known as Cluny III. It was once the largest church in the Christian world, headquarters of the powerful Benedictine order. Although essentially Romanesque in style, it features one of the earliest appearances of the pointed arch in Europe, imported from Syria, possibly via Amalfi Cathedral (see p. 274). Cluny Abbey's power and influence across Europe led to the pointed arch being incorporated into Christian architecture, and it became a central feature of the Gothic style.

LEFT

**PIERRE LOTI'S HOUSE, ROCHEFORT, FRANCE** (19TH C)

Pierre Loti was a naval officer and one of 19th-century France's most well-known and successful authors. He collected objects from his travels and used them in the creation of rooms in his house that evoked the countries he had visited and written about. One such room is designed like a mosque-mausoleum fantasy, with an Iznik-tile mihrab, horseshoe arches and five ceremoniously draped coffins. Loti's first novel, *Aziyadé*, is set in Istanbul, and there is a Piyerloti Hill in the Eyüp district of the city.

RIGHT

**ISLAMIC FUNERAL PAVILION, AMSTERDAM MUNICIPAL CEMETERY, THE NETHERLANDS** (2012)

This modest single-storey funeral building is located next to the largest Islamic burial ground in the Netherlands, which serves all the different Muslim communities in Amsterdam. The entrance features a full-height geometric composition made of individual cast-concrete elements that slot together, designed by Rem Posthuma. The composition wraps around the corner, giving it a surprisingly tactile three-dimensionality. The rear of the building has large glass doors that open on to the cemetery garden, its axis oriented towards Mecca. It was designed by architects PUUUR.

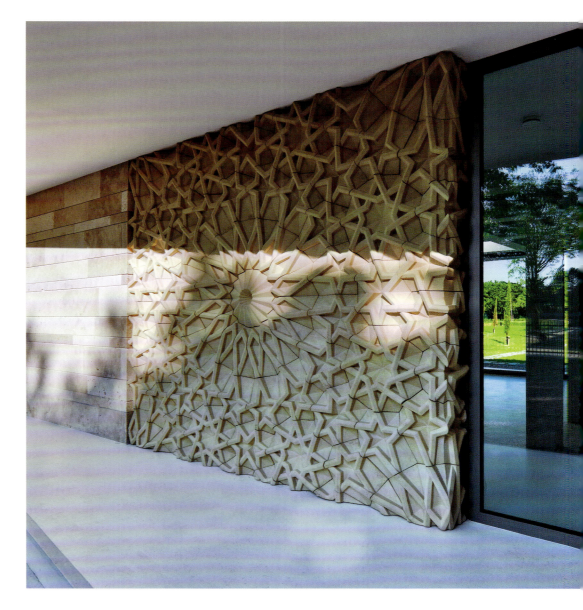

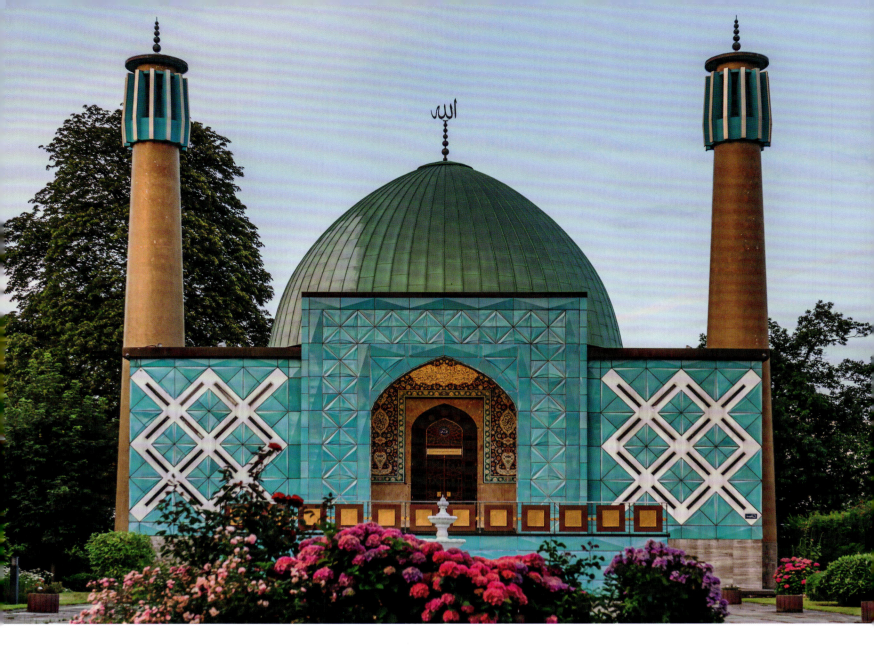

**IMAM ALI MOSQUE, HAMBURG, GERMANY** (1965)

One of the oldest mosques in Germany, it started as an idea discussed in 1953 by a group of Iranian businessmen in Hamburg. Funding was obtained from Iran and work started on the mosque in 1961, although it took almost two decades for it to achieve the finished appearance it has now. Many senior Iranian clergy and politicians, including an imam who later became president of Iran, have studied and worked at the mosque.

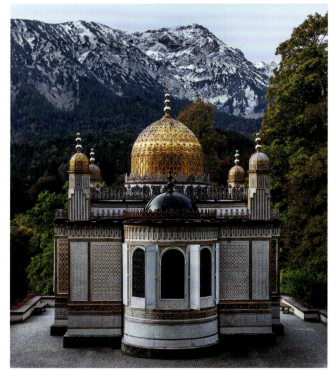

LEFT

**MOORISH KIOSK, SCHLOSS LINDERHOF, BAVARIA, GERMANY** (1867)

Schloss Linderhof was one of three castles built by King Ludwig II of Bavaria in the late 19th century. The Moorish Kiosk was originally designed for the 1867 Paris World's Fair by Carl von Diebitsch. Ludwig added many decorative elements to the interior such as a marble fountain and a throne that features three full-size gilded cast-bronze peacocks with feathers made of Bavarian glass. Ludwig liked to sit on his throne, wearing a Turkish costume and drinking tea, with his servants 'dressed as Muslims'.

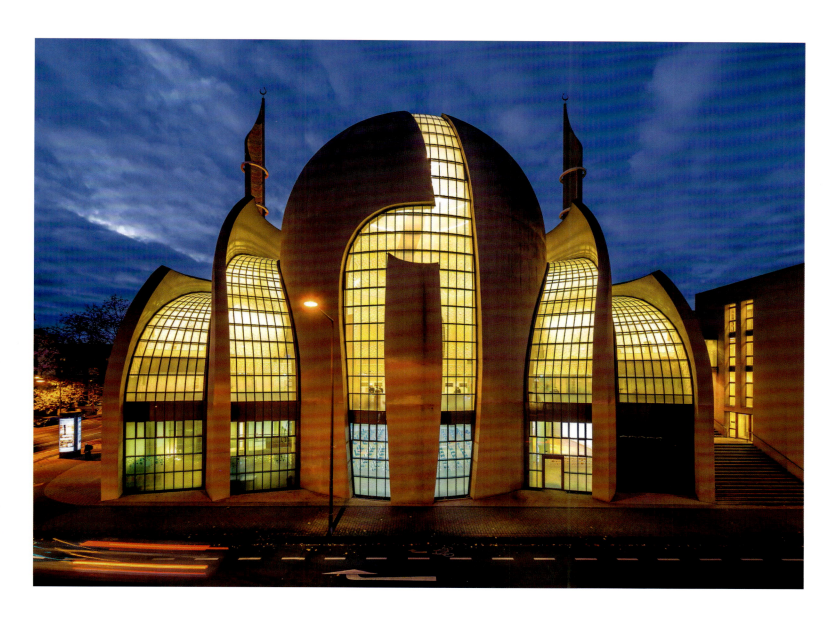

ABOVE

### CENTRAL MOSQUE, COLOGNE, GERMANY (2017)

The mosque's character emphasizes openness to the surrounding area: large glass walls enable passers-by to observe Muslims praying. Facilities open to all, such as restaurants, shops and event spaces, provide opportunity for non-Muslims to engage with the building and the communities who use it. The main dome is 26 m (85 ft) in diameter and 34.5 m (113 ft) high, and made of lightweight concrete. It was designed by Gottfried Böhm and his son Paul Böhm, who specialize in church architecture.

RIGHT

### GROSSES SCHAUSPIELHAUS, BERLIN, GERMANY (1919)

With seating for 3,500 people, this theatre was built in a repurposed building for impresario Max Reinhardt by architect Hans Poelzig. The cavernous interior space was painted red. The columns and domes were covered in thousands of muqarnas elements. The Nazis disapproved of the space and its shows; they took over the theatre and put in a hung ceiling to hide the muqarnas. The building was demolished in 1988.

**YENIDZE TOBACCO AND CIGARETTE FACTORY, DRESDEN, GERMANY** (1909)

In the early 20th century in central Dresden it was forbidden to build factories that looked like factories. Jewish entrepreneur Hugo Zietz came up with the idea of building his factory to look like a mosque, thereby echoing the origins of the Turkish tobacco in his products. One of the first things early 20th-century train travellers entering Dresden would have seen was 'Salem Aleikum' ('peace be upon you') in huge illuminated letters on the side of the factory – the brand of cigarettes produced there. Designed by architect Martin Hammitzsch, the building was one of the first in Europe to use the new ferroconcrete frame construction method. The minaret is in fact the chimney for the factory. The dome measures 20 m (66 ft) in height and is made entirely of coloured glass.

**RIJEKA ISLAMIC CENTRE, CROATIA** (2013)
The centre is sited on a large platform
overlooking the Croatian port of Rijeka. The
dome consists of six concrete segments
covered in steel plates that work together
to create a coherent structure. Below the
platform on which the dome rests are two
large storeys where most of the centre's
facilities are located, including a restaurant.
The centre is popular with locals, Muslim
and non-Muslim alike. It was conceived
by prominent Croatian sculptor Dušan
Džamonja, whose aim was to design a
mosque that looked like a sculpture.

**KUŠLAT MOSQUE, ZVORNIK, BOSNIA
AND HERZEGOVINA** (1451–1481)
Built during the reign of Sultan Mehmed
II, it is one of the oldest mosques in Bosnia
and Herzegovina. A fortress existed in this
location from before Ottoman times, and
the mosque was built for the Ottoman
troops stationed there. The mosque looks
like a house: only the wooden minaret
indicates the religious purpose of the
building. It was damaged during the war
in 1993 but has since been restored.

**KASIM-KATIB MOSQUE, SARAJEVO,
BOSNIA AND HERZEGOVINA** (1546)
Wooden minarets are generally rare, but not
in Bosnia and Herzegovina: a 1933 survey
found that of the 1,120 mosques, 786 had
wooden minarets. Most of them start from
the ceiling beams under the roof and rise to
between 10 and 15 m (33 and 50 ft) above the
ground. Kasim-Katib Mosque is considered
to be one of the most beautiful mosques
with a wooden minaret in Sarajevo. Nothing
is known about the history of the mosque.
It was destroyed during the sack of Sarajevo
by the Habsburg imperial army in 1697,
and reconstructed at the beginning of the
18th century.

BELOW

**KRUSZYNIANY MOSQUE, PODLASKIE VOIVODESHIP, POLAND** (2ND HALF 18TH C)

Muslims in Poland generally trace their heritage back to the Tatars in the 14th century, who arrived from Central Asia. Over the centuries, the Lipka Tatar population in Poland grew, and it is estimated that by the late 16th century there were around 400 mosques. After World War II, only two Tatar villages remained (Bohoniki and Kruszyniany). Kruszyniany Mosque is built of wood, with two towers, in the style of local churches. It is painted green, the colour associated with Islam. A mosque in this village was first mentioned in 1717. The current mosque was built later on the same site.

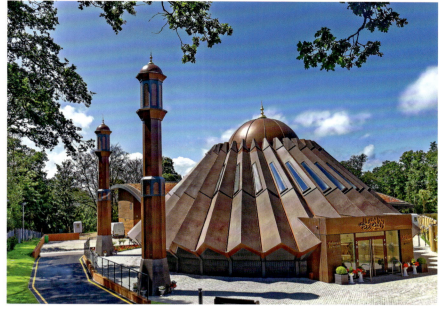

LEFT

**ARAB ROOM, CARDIFF CASTLE, WALES** (1881)

Cardiff Castle was remodelled for its owner, the 3rd Marquess of Bute, by architect and medieval revivalist William Burges. For the spectacular Arab Room, two floors were removed to create the required height. The most eyecatching feature is the oversized muqarnas ceiling, entirely covered in gold leaf – not just gold paint.

ABOVE

**MUBARAK MOSQUE, TILFORD, ENGLAND** (2019)

The mosque is on the site of the international headquarters of the Ahmadiyya Muslim Community and can accommodate 500 worshippers. The mosque's distinctive copper-clad roof is shaped from thirty-two angled creases that all lean in the same direction. They are equally visible on the inside. Other buildings in the complex include an equestrian centre, a sports hall, administrative buildings and thirty-three residences.

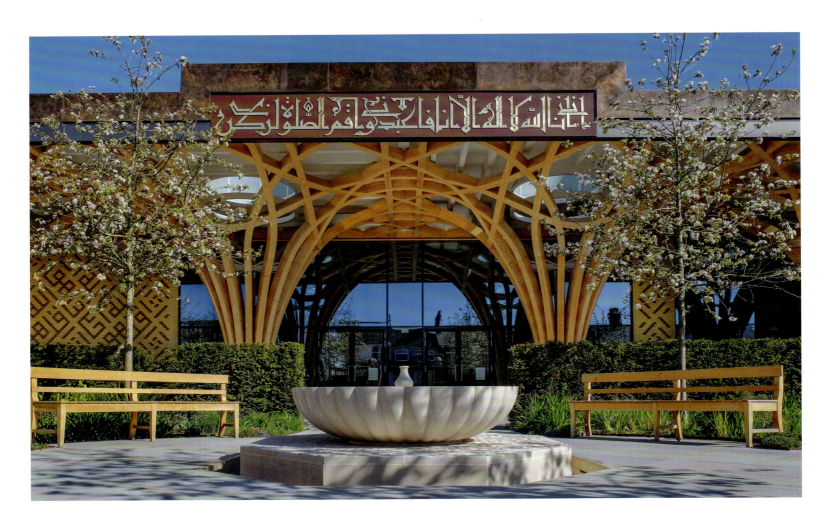

**CAMBRIDGE CENTRAL MOSQUE,
ENGLAND** (2019)

Opened in 2019, it is Cambridge's first purpose-built mosque. Its defining timber columns support the roof in an interlaced vault structure. Made of laminated spruce, they visually echo the famous Gothic fan vault at nearby King's College Chapel. Partial brickwork patterns on exterior and interior walls create the name of Allah and other religious phrases, reminiscent of Central Asian brickwork design. It was designed by architects Marks Barfield.

ABOVE

**EDINBURGH CENTRAL MOSQUE,
SCOTLAND** (1998)

Combining elements of Islamic architecture and Scottish baronial architecture, it is one of the first mosques in the UK to define itself both in reference to Islamic architecture and to the urban historical context in which it is located. As such, it can be seen as a trendsetter for mosque architecture in the UK. It was designed by architect Basil Al Bayati.

BELOW

**MALMÖ MOSQUE, SWEDEN** (1984)

It is one of the first mosques in Scandinavia. The initiative for its construction came from a language teacher from present-day Macedonia who moved to Sweden in the 1960s. He remained leader of the mosque and its school for over thirty years. The 1960s and 70s saw migrants from Yugoslavia and Turkey arrive in Western and Northern Europe, invited by governments and businesses, giving rise to a need for places of worship. The mosque has been expanded but, even so, is now too small for the Muslim community of Malmö. The architect was Jens Danstrup Jørgensen.

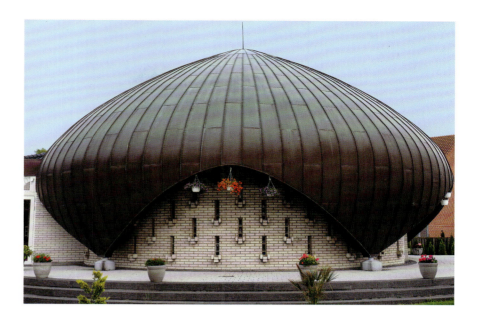

ABOVE

**NUSRAT DJAHAN MOSQUE, COPENHAGEN, DENMARK** (1967)

Financed entirely by female members of the worldwide Ahmadiyya communities, it was Denmark's first mosque. Designed by John Zachariassen, it was inspired by Walter Gropius's unbuilt mosque for Baghdad University. The dome was initially covered with azure ceramic tiles, which were later replaced by copper cladding. It was also supposed to have had a minaret, but the architect later considered it to be out of proportion to the suburban neighbourhood in which it is situated.

**ISLAMIC CULTURAL CENTER OF NEW YORK, NEW YORK CITY, USA** (1991)
This was the first mosque to be purpose-built for the Muslim community of New York. Its large square prayer hall is light, sparse and serene. The entire mosque is contained in a large imaginary cube that is subdivided into smaller cubes on a 5 x 5 x 5 grid. The interior and exterior are characterized by strong square forms in granite, combined with translucent glass elements etched with patterns, such as in the mihrab. The mosque is angled at 29 degrees to the dominant Manhattan street grid, so that the mihrab can face Mecca. It was designed by modernist architects Skidmore, Owings & Merrill.

OPPOSITE

**PENTHOUSE SUITE, FAIRMONT HOTEL, SAN FRANCISCO, CALIFORNIA, USA** (1926)
Taking up the entire eighth floor of one of San Francisco's most expensive hotels, the luxury suite has been used by John F. Kennedy, Alfred Hitchcock, Mick Jagger and many other politicians and celebrities. It incorporates a sixty-seat dining room, three huge bedrooms, a two-storey library, a living room with grand piano, and, famously, a Persian-style billiard room (left) designed by Persian-art expert Arthur Upham Pope.

RIGHT

**DAR AL-ISLAM MOSQUE, ABIQUIÚ, NEW MEXICO, USA** (1981)
The building was part of a planned Islamic community in the 1970s consisting of about fifty families. Today, the mosque and madrasa remain and Dar al-Islam is an educational centre for Muslims and non-Muslims alike. Both buildings are constructed of adobe and use the same architectural language of barrel vaults, half-domes, adobe screens and pointed arches. The buildings were designed by Egyptian architect Hassan Fathy, known for pioneering the use of appropriate materials, especially adobe in Egypt. The climate of New Mexico is similar to Egypt's, and earthen architecture is the local building tradition, just as it is around Luxor, Egypt.

BELOW

**MARIN COUNTY CIVIC CENTER, SAN RAFAEL, CALIFORNIA, USA** (1962)
This was Frank Lloyd Wright's largest public project, although construction started after his death. While working on designs for this project in the late 1950s, he was also working on a project in Baghdad (never built). The influence of Islamic architecture is clearly visible in the many arches and the domed structure of the Marin County library building and its adjacent spire, reminiscent as they are of a mosque dome and minaret.

RIGHT

### MEDINAH TEMPLE, CHICAGO, ILLINOIS, USA (1912)

Built by the Shriners (a US Masonic society), the Medinah Temple was primarily an auditorium with over 4,000 seats, and is considered to be one of the finest Moorish Revival Shriner 'temples' in the USA. Its distinctive onion domes, horseshoe arches, and ceramic and terracotta decorations have led to its being designated an official Chicago Landmark. Around the main entrance Arabic calligraphy repeats *'La ilaha illa Allah'* ('There is no God but Allah'). The building reopened as a department store in 2003 but was sold in 2020. It was designed by Chicago architects Huehl and Schmid.

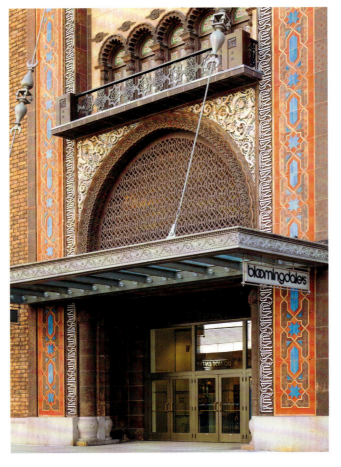

ABOVE & OPPOSITE

### THANKS-GIVING CHAPEL, DALLAS, TEXAS, USA (1976)

The interfaith chapel is the central focus in Thanks-Giving Square in the heart of Dallas. Designed by modernist architect Philip Johnson, the square was the initiative of local businessmen who wanted to create a public space dedicated to universal spiritual values. The chapel resembles the spiral Abbasid minarets of the Great Mosque of Samarra (see p. 66) and Abu Dulaf Mosque. Between the spiral walls is a large horizontal stained-glass composition by famed French artist Gabriel Loire.

## OPA-LOCKA, FLORIDA, USA (1926)

The city of Opa-Locka was founded by aviation pioneer Glenn Curtiss, who had a fondness for themes from *One Thousand and One Nights*. (The silent Hollywood film *The Thief of Bagdad* had come out in 1924.) Street names include Ali Baba Avenue, Harem Avenue and Aladdin Street. The city is the greatest agglomeration of Moorish Revival architecture in the western hemisphere. The skyline of the city was dominated by minarets, domes and crenellations. Architect Bernhardt Muller, who had never visited a Middle Eastern or North African country, designed 105 such buildings in Opa-Locka. The crowning jewel is City Hall, seen here, with double pink domes, pink and white 'ablaq' striping and a minaret.

**BAITUL ISLAM MOSQUE, VAUGHAN,
ONTARIO, CANADA** (1992)

For the first six years, this mosque run by the
Ahmadiyya Muslim Community stood alone
in a remote field north of Toronto, struggling
to attract the faithful. Now, hundreds of
homes have been purpose-built for this
community, called Peace Village. Residents
live within walking distance of the mosque.
Designed by Dr Gulzar Haider, it is one of
Canada's largest mosques.

**URSULINE PALACE, HAVANA, CUBA** (1913)
Built in the neo-Mudejar style by architect José Toraya, it especially borrows visual elements from the Great Mosque of Córdoba (see pp. 247 and 250–52), such as intersecting arches and horseshoe arches. The order of Ursuline nuns came to Cuba from New Orleans in the early 19th century, after Spain ceded Louisiana back to France. Their prosperous convent in Havana was dedicated to the education of youth.

**MOHAMMED VI CENTER FOR THE DIALOGUE OF CIVILIZATIONS, COQUIMBO, CHILE** (2007)

Its distinctive minaret rises high over its surroundings and is a copy of the famous minaret of the Kutubiyya Mosque in Marrakech (see p. 169). The centre is a joint project between the local municipality and the kingdom of Morocco. It has a library and a mosque and offers information on Islam and on Moroccan culture. Craftspeople from Fes spent three months creating the delicately carved plaster interior. It features painted wooden ceilings and doors, all imported from Morocco.

OPPOSITE

**CHURCH OF SANTO DOMINGO, QUITO, ECUADOR** (1650)

Intricately crafted wooden geometric ceilings are known in Spanish as *artesonados*. Quito has two of the most magnificent *artesonados* in South America (the other is in the Church of San Francisco). Both were completed in the 17th century. The plans and models for such ceilings came from various sources but it seems the work was done by local craftsmen. It is thought that there were once many dozens of *artesonados* in churches and monasteries across the Americas.

**FRIDAY MOSQUE OF YAZD, IRAN** (1324)
A woman is seen here praying while kneeling in a *gudal*. This is a feature of Shia mosques from the Safavid era. It is a shallow, recessed area in which the imam stands during a service to ensure that he is no higher than any of the other faithful in the prayer hall.

# Women in Islamic Architecture

Whenever women commissioned buildings, they were typically members of the ruling class and commissioned religious buildings: mosques, madrasas, mausolea and *khanqah*s (places of Sufi retreat). Often it was the mother of the sultan who had the power, influence, money and freedom to do so. Daughters of sultans were also known to commission buildings. They were frequently married to governors or viziers with whom the sultan wanted to build an alliance, and had a wedding dowry of which they seemed to keep personal control. Usually a father is mentioned in the dedication inscriptions of buildings, but not a husband.

In pre-Ottoman Anatolia, approximately 20 per cent of all funerary structures were dedicated to women. Of around a hundred madrasas built between the 12th and 15th centuries in Anatolia, five bear the names of women, three of whom were the mothers of sultans. Around 7 per cent of Ottoman mosques in and around Istanbul were built for or by women. Nine per cent of the buildings designed or renovated by the great Ottoman architect Mimar Sinan (*c.* 1490–1588) were commissioned by or dedicated to women. Even though these percentages might not seem so large, they are significant when it is considered that women had no public roles and that these architectural projects required large sums of money and were often political in their nature. Of the 30,000 waqf (charitable endowment; see pp. 320–21) documents audited in 1930s Turkey, 2,300 were registered to institutions that belonged to women. Of the almost 500 Ottoman drinking fountains that still existed in Istanbul in the 1930s, nearly 30 per cent were registered under waqfs that were established by women.

In Yemen, the Rasulid dynasty ruled from 1229 to 1454. Rasulid history shows that women in the ruling family were in positions to wield great political power, typically behind the scenes. They were also financially independent. During the Rasulid era, 150 religious institutions were built, mostly in the two main cities of Taiz and Zabid. One third of these were commissioned by women. These were mosques, *sabil*s (public drinking fountains), madrasas and *khanqah*s. Female patrons are documented as helping out financially to enable the completion of a project or the supervision of the construction of public roads.

Rasulid sultans also married the daughters of Sufi sheikhs and scholars. One such daughter was Jihat Salah, who built three madrasas, a mosque and a *khanqah*. Members of her entourage also commissioned the construction of religious buildings: there are three small mosques in Zabid that were built by slave women.

### Queen Zubaydah (762–831 CE; ABBASID)

Zubaydah was passionate about the welfare of the pilgrims who took the road from Kufa in Iraq to Mecca. She built wells, water tanks, pavements, palaces and resthouses all along the 1,400 km (870 mile)-long route, which eventually became known as the Darb Zubaydah (*darb* means 'road'). She reportedly spent a huge fortune on bringing water to Mecca by building a 27 km (17 mile) aqueduct in Mecca. She was married to Abbasid caliph Harun al-Rashid.

### Fatima and Maryam al-Fihriya al-Qurashiya (800–880 CE; IDRISID)

Daughters of a wealthy merchant from Kairouan (Qayrawan) in present-day Tunisia, they emigrated with their family to the newly established city of Fes in Morocco. After their father died when they were in their late fifties, it is claimed the sisters used their inheritance to pay for the construction of two mosques: Fatima built al-Qarawiyyin and Maryam al-Andalus, one on each side of the river. Al-Qarawiyyin developed into an important centre of learning, often considered to be one of the world's oldest universities.

### Queen Arwa bint Ahmad al-Sulayhi (*c.* 1048–1138; SULAYHID)

Arwa ruled the Sulayhid state, in historical Yemen, for over fifty years. She moved the capital from Sana'a to Jibla and built a new palace. The old palace of Jibla was transformed into the mosque where she would finally be buried (see p. 59). She commissioned various other projects in Jibla: bathhouses, bridges, roads, aqueducts and mosques. She is remembered fondly by Yemenis as Bilqis al-Sughra, the 'Little Queen of Sheba'.

Queen Arwa was exceptional in many ways, not least because of the fact that the Friday prayers (*khutba*) were said in her name in the mosques of Yemen during her reign. No woman in the Arab world since has had this honour. During her reign Isma'ili missionaries were sent to western India, where a major Isma'ili centre was established in Gujarat (which continues to be a stronghold of the Isma'ili Bohra faith). The Sulayhids had two queens: Arwa's mother-in-law, Asma, ruled before her.

### Terkan Khatun (1053–1094; GREAT SELJUK)

Terkan Khatun was patron of the famous and architecturally important north dome of the

ABOVE

**MIHRIMAH SULTAN**

Mihrimah Sultan was a popular subject for painters in the 16th century. This one after Cristofano dell'Altissimo (c. 1530–1605), is titled *Cameria, Daughter of the Emperor Soliman*. 'Mihrimah' means 'sun and moon' in Persian. In the West she was known as Cameria, a version of *qamariah*, 'of the moon'.

OVERLEAF

**NUR JAHAN**

The are many paintings of Nur Jahan, and she is typically portrayed as wearing many pearls and other jewels. In this late 18th-century painting, made in the city of Bikaner, Rajasthan, her fingertips are henna-stained and she holds a gold cup and flask.

Friday Mosque of Isfahan (see pp. 72–73). When the 14th-century scholar and explorer Ibn Battuta travelled through the Mongol Empire and visited Turkic courts (such as that of the Great Seljuks), he was surprised by the role of women in public life and in politics. It was different from what he was used to in Arab societies. Terkan Khatun was the wife of Malik Shah, sultan of the Great Seljuks. After the death of her husband in 1092, she in effect took charge of the enormous empire.

**Gevher Nesibe** (D. 1206; ANATOLIAN SELJUK)
The Seljuks' first medical institution, in Kayseri, Turkey, was built in honour of Gevher Nesibe by her brother, Sultan Kaykhusraw I, respecting her final wish before she died. According to legend, she had been in love with a cavalry officer but her brother objected and sent the officer on dangerous missions to hasten his demise. Overcome with grief, Gevher Nesibe became ill and doctors were unable to heal her. Completed in 1210, the Gevher Nesibe hospital was one of the most modern medical complexes of its time, combining a hospital and medical school, as well as, reportedly, a psychiatric ward where patients were treated with music therapy. It continued to serve as a teaching hospital until the late 19th century.

**Dhayfa Khatun** (1185–1242; AYYUBID)
Dhayfa was a prominent architectural patron, establishing many outstanding buildings in Aleppo, Syria. Her father was the brother of Saladin and she married a son of Saladin. She became Queen of Aleppo when her son died and her grandson was still too young to rule. She commissioned two exceptional madrasas in the city: al-Firdaus Madrasa (Paradise School), and the Khankah School.

**Melike Mama Hatun** (12TH–13TH C; SALTUKID)
Ruler of the Saltukid dynasty from 1191 to 1200, Mama Hatun commissioned many significant buildings in the city of Tercan in the eastern Anatolia region of Turkey, including a caravanserai, a mosque, a bridge and a hammam. Locals still call the city Mamahatun. (See p. 114.)

**Shajar al-Durr** (D. 1257; MAMLUK)
Shajar al-Durr was the first ruler of the Mamluk Empire, albeit only for the summer of 1250. She was a powerful presence in Cairo for several decades as the wife of two consecutive sultans. In architecture, she started a new tradition by building the first combined madrasa-mausoleum. Attaching a mausoleum to a madrasa, mosque or *khanqah* became characteristic of Mamluk architecture. She inspired other female Mamluk patrons to construct similar buildings. She also broke with tradition by building the first royal mausoleum within the city of Cairo rather than outside the city. She died in 1257, killed on the instructions of the mother of her successor, Ali. (Umm Ali, meaning 'mother of Ali', is also the name of Egypt's most popular dessert; legend has it that she created it to celebrate the death of Shajar al-Durr.)

**Turan Malik** (13TH C; MENGUJEK)
Famous for her generosity and philanthropy, she used all her wealth in the construction of the masterpiece *darussifa* (hospital), which is part of the complex of the Great Mosque and Hospital of Divriği (see p. 117). Her father was the Mengujek ruler of Erzincan in eastern Turkey, Fakr al-Din Bahramshah (1162–1225).

**Mahperi Huand Hatun** (13TH C; GREAT SELJUK)
Mahperi Huand Hatun commissioned the Hunat Hatun complex in Kayseri, Turkey (1238), its buildings exquisitely decorated in carved stone with geometric patterns and floral themes. With its hammam, mosque, madrasa and mausoleum, it was the first multi-use complex built by the Anatolian Seljuks. She also built a series of caravanserais. Thought to have been Greek or Armenian, she was the daughter of the ruler of Kalonoros, whose city the Seljuks captured in 1221.

She became the first wife of Seljuk ruler Alladin Kayqubad I. All her architectural commissions were made during the reign of her son, not of her husband.

**Turabek Khanum** (14TH C; GOLDEN HORDE)
Turabek Khanum was responsible for the construction of the Friday Mosque of Konye-Urgench, Turkmenistan, which no longer exists. (See p. 156 for her mausoleum.) She was famous in her lifetime as a builder and a patron of the arts and of Islam and its institutions. Ibn Battuta met her (he failed to recognize her in the street). She was the daughter of Uzbek Khan (r. 1313–41), who brought Islam to Central Asia. Various versions of a legend are related in Central Asia: the princess and the builder (or slave). One version starts with a sheikh riding a donkey past a mausoleum that Turabek is building for herself. He asks if she will sell it to him. She replies jokingly: only if it were filled with gold! A friend of the sheikh climbs on to the dome, and shakes his right sleeve over the hole in the ceiling, and gold pours out until the mausoleum is filled. Turabek then has to sell her mausoleum, and laments that there will now be nothing to remember her by. In tears, she falls asleep and in her dreams sees a wonderful building in paradise. She uses the gold to construct this building from her dreams; it takes seven years. One builder, Quli Gardan, refuses to be paid in gold but instead wants Turabek's love. She replies that if he really loved her, he would jump off the building. He does; he dies. She holds his head in her lap and says, 'We will see you in the next world.' Bibi Khanum, Timur's wife, is the subject of a similar legend, possibly transmitted via the builders from Konye-Urgench who were forced to work on Timur's monuments in Samarkand after he had conquered their city.

**Queen Gawhar Shad** (D. 1457; TIMURID)
Gawhar Shad became de facto ruler of the Timurid Empire when her husband of sixty years, Shah Rukh (son of Timur) died in 1447. She famously ignored the tradition that only male rulers could commission the construction of prestigious Friday mosques by building the Friday Mosque of Herat (Afghanistan; see pp. 154–55) and the Friday Mosque of Mashhad (Iran; see opposite). Gawhar Shad paid for the mosques with her own money. They are now considered to represent Timurid architecture at its finest and most majestic. They were both built by the most celebrated architect of his time, Qawam al-Din Shirazi.

**Hürrem Sultan** (1500–1558; OTTOMAN)
She sponsored Mimar Sinan's first project as imperial architect, the Hürrem Sultan complex in Istanbul, as well as four schools in Mecca and the Haseki Sultan complex in Jerusalem. Wife of Süleyman the Magnificent and mother of Mihrimah Sultan (see below), she was known in the West as Roxelana.

**Bega Begum** (C. 1511–1582; MUGHAL)
She commissioned the first Mughal garden tomb on the Indian subcontinent for Emperor Humayun, her husband, on his death in 1556. When he died after falling down the stairs from his library, clutching a pile of books, she was so bereft that she could only dedicate herself to the construction of this imposing mausoleum. It is considered an early masterpiece of Mughal architecture and had a profound influence on later designs, not least on that of the Taj Mahal. Bega Begum also built a madrasa near the tomb.

**Mihrimah Sultan** (1522–1578; OTTOMAN)
The endowment deed of the Mihrimah Sultan Mosque in Üsküdar, Istanbul, demonstrates her status, referring to her as 'the sultan's favoured daughter, [...] a Fatima in innocence, a Khadija in chastity, an Aisha in intelligence, a Bilqis in natural disposition, and the Rabi'a of the epoch' (Fatima is the daughter of the Prophet, Khadija the first wife of the Prophet, Aisha the most beloved wife of the Prophet, Bilqis the Queen of Sheba,

Rabi'a an 8th-century Sufi mystic). Mihrimah was the daughter of Hürrem Sultan (see above) and Süleyman the Magnificent. She married the vastly wealthy Rüstem Pasha, grand vizier to her father. The construction of Rüstem Pasha's mosque, built after his death, was largely overseen by Mihrimah.

**Empress Nur Jahan** (1577–1645; MUGHAL)
Renowned for her passion for art, jewelry and dress styles, she effectively ruled the empire while her husband, Emperor Jahangir, was afflicted by various addictions. The prosperity of the Mughal court attracted craftsmen from Persia, Central Asia and Southern Asia, who were given artistic freedom to make works of the highest quality. Although Jahangir is commonly credited as making this artistic flowering possible, it is thought that the role of his Persian-born wife Nur Jahan was essential. She built a *sarai* (resting place or inn) in Jalandhar that was so large and impressive that any imposing building in the region was thence called Sarai Nur Mahal.

# A Waqf

A waqf is a charitable endowment under Islamic law. It usually involves the donation of a building or a plot of land and its assets for charitable purposes. The income it generates is used to support charitable and educational institutions and is often exempt from taxation. It is intended to be perpetual. Religious and educational institutions can be built, elaborately embellished and provided with a reliable source of revenue thanks to this system. The waqf system plays a central role across the Islamic world. Waqf documents typically contain detailed information and are, as such, very valuable to historians.

Many of the Timurid architectural masterpieces in Samarkand and Herat were made possible by the advantages of the waqf system. An insight into the system is offered by the poet, statesman and scholar Mir Ali Shir Nava'i, who was born in 1441 in Herat, the capital of the Timurid Empire. He is a much-loved historical figure; he popularized literature in the Turkic language (rather than Persian), much in the same way that Chaucer did for English and Dante for Italian. Over the course of his life in Herat, Nava'i worked as an official for the Timurid court and maintained a close friendship with the sultan. He used his influence and wealth to build mosques, schools, libraries and caravanserais in Khorasan province. His most famous projects are the mausoleum in Nishapur for the 13th-century poet Farad al-Din Attar (author of *The Conference of the Birds*) and the Ilkhlasiyya complex in Herat. Nava'i wrote a short work, *Vaqfiyya* (or *Waqfiya*), in 1481, about the latter. In it, he explains how he acquired the land for the complex, describes the layout and location of some of the buildings, lists the properties he converted into waqf and gives the conditions for their operation and maintenance. This was not a legal document (the official waqf documents, as well as the buildings have not survived); it was a way for Nava'i to have a record, a summary for himself. (One of the reasons it has survived is that it was frequently copied because it was seen as literary output by the great author.) It is a fascinating look into the practical processes of construction and of the waqf.

Ali Shir Nava'i writes that he was granted a tract of land in 1476/77 by his friend the Timurid sultan Husain Bayqara (r. 1469–1506), near a location called Kushk-i Marghani, to build himself a residence. He constructed several buildings, which he refers to as *qusur* (palaces). He enclosed 30 *jarib* (approximately 7.5 ha / 18½ acres) with a wall and cultivated the land. He writes: 'I made its *baghcha* (orchard/garden) beautiful with every sort of tree and adorned its *chaman* (meadows) with every sort of vegetation.' (Apparently, 'sons of emirs and princes' had tried to do the same in this area and had not been successful.) The Kushk-i Marghani was evidently an ancient structure, two storeys high, made of stone and unbaked brick. Nava'i describes it as a monastery-like building, with a foundation resembling a church (it was probably a Nestorian Christian church and monastery). He demolished it so he could build his mosque (which he calls Qudsiyya Mosque) and madrasa (which he calls Ilkhlasiyya Madrasa, because he built it 'out of pure sincerity', *khulus-i ilklasdin*). He built a *khanqah* opposite the madrasa, along the Injil Canal, which runs all the way to the Gawhar Shad Mausoleum. He named the *khanqah* Khalasiyya because it was a building free of ostentation and pretence, that freed (*khalas berdi*) the mind from its troubles. He built these structures as his private property, but later transferred them to a charitable waqf foundation as a way to ensure their continuity.

In a waqf document, the endower is entitled to specify how income from the foundation is to be spent. Ali Shir Nava'i lists all his properties; the income they generate is to be mostly spent on his madrasa and *khanqah*. He categorizes the properties according to whether they are in Herat or outside Herat. He has twenty-six commercial properties, including the skullcap sellers' market building and a shop called The Water Jug. The majority of his properties are outside Herat. They include orchards, vineyards, wheatfields, irrigation canals, a village and several hamlets.

Ali Shir Nava'i stipulates that a 'sweet-voiced' imam and 'mellifluous-sounding' *muqri* (Quran reader) should be appointed. For the madrasa, two scholars were to be appointed, one to lecture on *fiqh* (Islamic jurisprudence), the other on *hadith* (the traditions of the Prophet). There were to be two *halqa* (study circles) of eleven students each. Six *hafiz* (Quran reciters) were to be appointed to read the Quran in the specially constructed domed chamber in the madrasa, the Dar al-Huffaz. The *khanqah* was home to Sufi dervishes; its primary function was to distribute food to the poor every day. Nava'i stipulated that the *khanqah* had to have a *tabbakh* (cook), a *tabaqchi* (server), a *farrash* (concierge), and two *khadim* (servants). He even specified quantities of food and types of dishes that normally had to be served and what to serve on special occasions (such as the first day of the new academic year, the anniversary of the birth of the Prophet, and each night of the month of Ramadan). The *Vaqfiyya* also makes provision for the annual purchase of clothes for the poor: 100 fur-lined garments, 100 woollen cloaks, 100 sheepskin caps, 100 pairs of shoes, 100 shirts and 100 pairs of trousers. These were to be distributed in consultation with the two scholars of the madrasa. A preacher, an imam and a Quran reader were also to be appointed to the *khanqah*. Apparently the locals made 'every conceivable excuse' not to make the trip to the mosque, so they would now be able to perform their prayers in the *khanqah*, which was in the middle of their neighbourhood.

As is customary, the entire waqf was to be managed by a *mutavalli* (trustee), aided by a financial officer and a chief intendant. The trustee had to hire two 'sturdy aides' to help with the agricultural management. Most commonly, waqf management is hereditary, so the descendants of

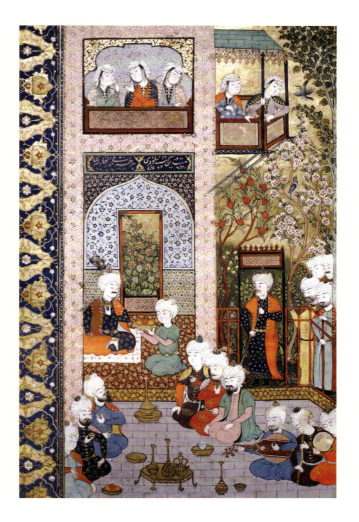

**A RULER HOLDS COURT** (16TH C)
Illustration from a *diwan*, or collection of poems, by Mir Ali Shir Nava'i whose four *diwans* each dealt with a different stage of life.

the first *mutavalli* have the same responsibilities and benefits for many generations. Salaries were paid out in cash and in kind. The highest paid was the *mutavalli*, who received 2,000 *altin* (gold coins) and twenty loads of grain. The lowest paid were the server, the concierge, two servants and the Quran reader at the *khanqah*: they received 200 *altin* and five loads of wheat. They were also responsible for clearing the snow in winter and dredging the canal. The *mutavalli* had 400 *altin* to spend each year on rugs, lighting and reed mats. Every thirty years, the *mutavalli* had to make a new copy of the waqf document. As is typical with waqf documents, it states that as long as the conditions set out in the documents are fulfilled, no government official or trustee should involve himself with the foundation's business nor take anything they are not entitled to. Waqf foundations had a great deal of fiscal immunity.

# Glossary

**ablaq** An architectural style with alternating rows of light and dark stone.

**adobe** A building material made from sand and clay mixed with organic matter such as straw and generally dried in the sun; bricks or buildings were made from such material.

**Ahmadiyya** An Islamic revival movement, originating in the 19th century in the Punjab region of India (now East and West Punjab).

**aina-kari** Geometric compositions made of small pieces of mirrored glass. Most commonly seen in Iran and Iraq, but also in India.

**al-Andalus** The area of the Iberian Peninsula (modern-day Portugal and Spain) that was under Muslim rule from 711 CE to 1492.

**bayt/beit** Arabic word for house.

**bismillah** The first word in the Quran, often spoken as a blessing (Arabic: 'in the name of Allah').

**Byzantine Empire** (395–1453) The continuation of the Roman Empire in its eastern half, which survived after the western half had fragmented; also known as the Eastern Roman Empire. Its capital was Constantinople (Istanbul).

**caravanserai** An inn accommodating travellers and their goods and animals, typically along the Silk Road and other trade routes across Asia and Africa. A composite Turkish/Persian word, consisting of *caravan* (group of travellers) and *serai* (palace).

**chahar bagh** A formal garden layout based on the four gardens of Paradise mentioned in the Quran, in which a garden is divided by four axial paths or water channels, creating four plots of equal shape and size.

**congregational mosque** See Friday mosque

**Coptic** Describing an Orthodox Christian community, the Copts, indigenous to North Africa and principally living in Egypt and Sudan.

**Crusader kingdoms/states** (1098–1291) The four states established in territories gained by the Crusades in the Middle East.

**Friday mosque/congregational mosque (*jami masjid*)** A mosque used by the entire community for Friday prayers, the most important weekly ritual in Muslim communities.

**gunbad** Persian term for a dome.

**Hajj** The pilgrimage made to the Kaaba in Mecca, a mandatory religious duty for Muslims, provided they are physically and financially able.

**hammam** A private or public bathhouse; also called a Turkish bath.

**haram** A private area of a house, or the sanctuary of a mosque.

**hazarbaf** Persian term for decorative brickwork.

**hypostyle mosque** A traditional mosque design that features a flat roof supported by columns.

**Ibadism** A school of Islam.

**imam** The prayer leader of a mosque.

**Isma'ilism** A branch of Shia Islam.

**iwan** A hall or other rectangular space with a vaulted ceiling and entirely open on one side.

**Iznik ceramics** Ottoman-era tiles, produced from the 1550s in the Turkish town of Iznik. The tiles are characterized by their distinctive underglaze blue and red and their floral designs.

**jali** A Mughal-era pierced stone screen, usually with a geometric design.

**khanqah** A place of retreat for Sufis.

**kiosk** Turkish term for a small pavilion.

**külliye** Turkish term for a complex around or next to a mosque that includes many different buildings, such as a madrasa, library, bathhouse, kitchen for the poor, *khanqah*.

**madrasa** A building that functions as a place of education, mostly in the Islamic sciences.

**malwiya** A spiral tower.

**maqsura** A screened-off area in front of the mihrab and minbar. It appears mostly in early mosques and was often used to give privacy to the sultan.

**maristan/bimaristan** A hospital providing a range of services, which often included a teaching school and carried out medical research.

**mashrabiyya** A wooden screen that covers a balcony or window, typically made of short pieces of turned wood joined together.

**medina** A term often used in North Africa to describe the old part of a city.

**mihrab** A niche, usually in a mosque, that indicates the direction of prayer.

**mimar** Turkish word for architect.

**minbar** The pulpit in a mosque from where the imam delivers his sermon.

**minaret** A tower attached to a mosque, from which Muslims are called to prayer.

**Mozarabic** Referring to Christians living under Muslim rule in al-Andalus.

**Mudejar** Referring to Muslims living under the rule of Christian monarchs in al-Andalus; and to the style of art and architecture that developed during this time.

**musalla** A place where prayer is performed.

**muqarnas** A system of small connected niches used to embellish entrances and create gradual transitions between the base of a dome and the walls it rests on.

**pishtaq** Persian term for an arched portal projecting from the façade of a building.

**qasr** An Islamic castle, fortress, palace or mansion.

**qibla** The direction towards Mecca, in which Muslims perform their prayers.

**riwaq** An arcade or portico, open on at least one side.

**sabil** A public drinking fountain.

**sabil-kuttab** a building with a public drinking fountain on the ground floor, and a *kuttab* (children's Quranic school) on the upper floor.

**sahn** The courtyard of a mosque.

**Sasanian (or Sassanid) Empire** (224–651) The last pre-Islamic empire in Iran and the longest-lived Iranian imperial dynasty.

**shabestan** An underground space. Iranian mosques may have them as summer prayer halls, especially in hot environments.

**spolia** Architectural fragments that are repurposed and reused in a new structure (Latin: 'spoils').

**squinch** A small arch in the corner of a building that creates a transition to an octagonal base for a dome.

**Sunni** The larger of the two main branches of Islam.

**Shia** The smaller of the two main branches of Islam.

**stucco** Decorative plasterwork in architecture.

**surah** A 'chapter' of the Quran, of which there are 114.

**toron** A projecting wooden stake in West African mud architecture.

**windcatcher** (Farsi *badgir*; Arabic *malqaf*) A tall, chimney-like structure that expels warm air during the day and catches cool air in the evening.

**ziyada** The open space between a mosque and its surrounding wall.

# Islamic Dynasties

This is a selective list, designed to help the reader to identify buildings within dynastic periods around the world. The dates given here – as elsewhere in the book – refer to the Common Era (CE) in the Gregorian calendar.

**Umayyad** (660–750) Capitals: Damascus, Harran

**Abbasid** (750–1258) Capitals: Kufa, Anbar, Baghdad, Raqqa, Samarra / (1261–1517) Capital: Cairo

**Umayyads** in Spain (756–1031) Capitals: Córdoba, Madinat al-Zahra

**Aghlabid** (800–909) Capital: Kairouan

**Samanid** (819–999) Capitals: Samarkand, Bukhara

**Taharid** (821–873) Capitals: Merv, Nishapur

**Qarakhanid** (840–1212) Capitals: Balasagun, Kashgar, Samarkand

**Tulunid** (868–905) Capital: al-Qata'i

**Ghurid** (c. 879–1215) Capitals: Firozkoh, Hrat, Ghazni

**Fatimid** (909–1171) Capitals: Raqqada, Mahdia, al-Mansuriya, Cairo

**Ziyarid** (931–1090) Capitals: Isfahan, Rayy, Gorgan, Amol

**Ghaznavid** (977–1186) Capitals: Ghazni, Lahore

**Great Seljuk** (1037–1194) Capitals: Nishapur, Rayy, Isfahan, Merv, Hamadan

**Sulayhid** (1047–1138) Capitals: Sana'a, Jibla

**Almoravid** (1050–1147) Capitals: Azougui, Aghmat, Marrakech

**Saltukid** (1071–1202) Capital: Erzerum

**Khwarazmian** (1077–1231) Capitals: Gurganj, Samarkand, Ghazna, Tabriz

**Anatolian Seljuk** (1081–1307) Capitals: Iznik, Konya, Sivas

**Artuqid** (1101–1409) Capitals: Hasankeyf, Diyarbakr, Harput, Mardin

**Almohad** (1121–1269) Capitals: Tinmel, Marrakech, Seville, Córdoba

**Zengid** (1127–1250) Capital: Damascus

**Norman Sicily** (1130–1194) Capital: Palermo

**Delhi Sultanate** (1206–1526) Capitals: Lahore, Badayun, Delhi, Daulatabad, Delhi, Agra

**Mongol** (1206–1638) Capitals: Avarga, Karakorum, Khanbaliq

**Chagatai-Khan** (1226–1347) Capitals: Almaliq, Karshi

**Golden Horde** (1227–1502) Capitals: Sarai, Sighnaq

**Rasulid** (1229–1454) Capital: Zabid

**Nasrid** (1230–1492) Capital: Granada

**Marinid** (1244–1465) Capital: Fes

**Karamanid** (1250–1487) Capitals: Larende, Ermenek, Konya, Mut, Eregli

**Mamluk** (1250–1517) Capital: Cairo

**Ilkhanid** (1256–1335) Capitals: Maaghh, Tabriz, Soltaniyeh

**Eshrefid** (1280–1326) Capital: Beysehir

**Ottoman** (1299–1922) Capitals: Sogut, Iznik, Bursa, Edirne, Istanbul

**Tughluqid** (1320–1414) Capital: Delhi

**Shah Mir** (1339–1561) Capital: Srinagar

**Bahmanid** (1347–1527) Capitals: Gulbarga, Bidar.

**Bengal Sultanate** (1352–1576) Capitals: Pandua, Gaur, Tanda

**Timurid** (1370–1507) Capitals: Samarkand, Herat

**Gujarat Sultanate** (1407–1573) Capitals: Anhilwad Patan, Ahmedabad, Muhammadabad

**Lodi dynasty** (1451–1526) Capital: Delhi

**Adil Shahi** (1489–1686) Capital: Bijapur

**Safavid** (1501–1736) Capitals: Tabriz, Qazvin, Isfahan

**Saadi** (1510–1659) Capitals: Tidsi, Afghan, Marrakech, Fes

**Khiva Khanate** (1511–1920) Capital: Khiva

**Mughal** (1526–1857) Capitals: Agra, Delhi, Lahore, Dhaka

**Janid** (1599–1747) Capital: Bukhara

**Alaouite** (1631–present) Capitals: Fes, Meknes

**Shaki Khanate** (1743–1819) Capital: Shaki

**Zand** (1751–1794) Capital: Shiraz

**Talpur dynasty** (1783–1843) Capitals: Hyderabad, Khairpur, Mirpur Khas

**Qajar** (1789–1925) Capital: Tehran

**Sokoto Caliphate** (1804–1903) Capital: Gudu, Sokoto, Birnin Konni, Burmi

# Bibliography

Agnello, Fabrizio, 'The Painted Ceiling of the Nave of the Capella Palatina in Palermo: An Essay on Its Geometric and Constructive Features', *Muqarnas*, vol. 27, 2010, pp. 407–47

Almagro, Antonio, 'La Puerta Califal del Castillo de Gormaz', *Arqueología de la Arquitectura*, 5, 2008, pp. 55–77

Angulo, Diego, and Helen B. Hall, 'The Mudejar Style in Mexican Architecture', *Ars Islamica*, vol. 2, no. 2, 1935, pp. 225–30

Apotsos, Michelle, 'New Meanings and Historical Messages in the Larabanga Mosque', *African Arts*, vol. 49, no. 4, 2016, pp. 8–23

Arbabzadah, Nushin, 'Women and Religious Patronage in the Timurid Empire' *in Afghanistan's Islam: From Conversion to the Taliban*, Nile Green (ed.), Oakland: University of California Press, 2017, pp. 56–70

Asher, Catherine Blanshard, *Architecture of Mughal India*, vol. 4, Cambridge; New York: Cambridge University Press, 1992

Badran, Rasem, 'A Trinity of Values in Architecture for Muslim Societies', *International Journal of Islamic Architecture*, vol. 10, no. 1, 2021, pp. 247–56

Bates, Ülkü, 'Women as Patrons of Architecture in Turkey', *Women in the Muslim World*, Cambridge, MA: Harvard University Press, 1978, pp. 245–60

Behrens-Abouseif, Doris, *Islamic Architecture in Cairo: An Introduction*, Cairo: AUC Press, 1989

Behrens-Abouseif, Doris, 'The Mahmal Legend and the Pilgrimage of the Ladies of the Mamluk Court', *Mamluk Studies Review 1*, 1997, pp. 87–96

Berlekamp, Persis, 'Symmetry, Sympathy, and Sensation: Talismanic Efficacy and Slippery Iconographies in Early Thirteenth-Century Iraq, Syria, and Anatolia', *Representations*, no. 133, 2016, pp. 59–109

Bierschenk, Thomas, 'Religion and Political Structure: Remarks on Ibadism in Oman and the Mzab (Algeria)', *Studia Islamica*, no. 68, 1988, pp. 107–27

Blair, Sheila S., 'The Mongol Capital of Sultāniyya, "The Imperial"', Iran, vol. 24, 1986, pp. 139–51

Blair, Sheila S., 'Muslim-style Mausolea across Mongol Eurasia: Religious Syncretism, Architectural Mobility and Cultural Transformation', *Journal of the Economic and Social History of the Orient*, vol. 62, nos 2–3, 2019, pp. 318–55

Blair, Sheila S., and Jonathan Bloom, 'From Iran to the Deccan: Architectural Transmission and the Madrasa Mahmud Gawan at Bidar' in K. Overton (ed.), *Iran and the Deccan: Persianate Art, Culture, and Talent in Circulation*, Bloomington: Indiana Universty Press, 2020, p. 175

Brooks, Jeffery R., 'From Azulejos to Zaguanes: The Islamic Legacy in the Built Environment of Hispano-America', *Journal of the Southwest*, vol. 45, no. 1/2, 2003, pp. 289–327

Bush, Olga, 'The Writing on the Wall: Reading the Decoration of the Alhambra', *Muqarnas*, vol. 26, 2009, pp. 119–47

Busquets, Eduardo Lopez, 'Andalusi and Mudejar art in its international scope: legacy and modernity', *Casa Arabe*, 2015

Capilla, Susana C., 'The Visual Construction of the Umayyad Caliphate in al-Andalus through the Great Mosque of Córdoba', *Arts*, vol. 7, no. 3, 2018, p. 36

Cataldi, Giancarlo, et al., 'The Town of Ghardaïa in M'zab, Algeria: Between Tradition and Modernity', *Traditional Dwellings and Settlements Review*, vol. 7, no. 2, 1996, pp. 63–74

Chida-Razvi, Mehreen, 'From Function to Form: Chini-khana in Safavid and Mughal Architecture', *South Asian Studies*, vol. 35, no. 1, 2019, pp. 82–106

Chmelnizkij, Sergei, 'The Mausoleum of Muhammad Bosharo', *Muqarnas*, vol. 7, no. 1, 1989, pp. 23–34

Çinar, Hande Sanem, and Funda Yirmibeşoğlu, 'The Architecture of Fauna in Turkey: Birdhouses', *Current Urban Studies*, vol. 7, no. 4, 2019, pp. 551–61

Citarella, Armand O., 'The Relations of Amalfi with the Arab World before the Crusades', *Speculum*, vol. 42, no. 2, 1967, pp. 299–312

Corsi, Andrea Luigi, and Martina Massullo, by email, unpublished research presented at the conference 'Dans l'objectif d'Henry Viollet: Les monuments islamiques à travers un fonds d'archives inexploré (1904–1913)', organized by Martina Massullo and Sandra Aube, Paris, 23 June 2022 (publication forthcoming)

Cousens, Henry, 'Bījāpūr and Its Architectural Remains: With an Historical Outline of the 'Ādil Shāhi Dynasty', Bombay: Government Central Press, 1916

Daftary, Farhad, and Sayyida Hurra, 'The Isma'ili Sulayhid Queen of Yemen', in *Women in the Medieval Islamic World: Power, Patronage and Piety*, Gavin R. G. Hambly (ed.), London: St Martin's Press, 1998

Dale, Stephen Frederic, 'The Legacy of the Timurids', Journal of the *Royal Asiatic Society*, vol. 8, no. 1, 1998, pp. 43–58

Darke, Diana, *Stealing from the Saracens: How Islamic Architecture Shaped Europe*, London: Hurst & Company, 2020

De Montéquin, François-Auguste, 'Arches in the Architecture of Muslim Spain: Typology and Evolution', *Islamic Studies*, vol. 30, no. 1/2, 1991, pp. 67–82

Di Liberto, Rosa, 'Norman Palermo: Architecture between the 11th and 12th Century', in A. Nef, *A Companion to Medieval Palermo*, Leiden; Boston: Brill, 2013, pp. 139–94

Dodds, Jerrilynn D., 'Mudejar tradition and the Synagogues of Medieval Spain: Cultural Identity and Cultural Hegemony', in V. B. Mann, T. F. Glick and J. D. Dodds (eds), *Convivencia: Jews, Muslims and Christians in Medieval Spain*, New York: Jewish Museum, 1992

El-Shorbagy, Abdel-Moniem (2020) 'Women in Islamic Architecture: Towards Acknowledging their Role in the Development of Islamic Civilization', *Cogent Arts & Humanities*, vol. 7, no. 1, article: 1741984

Fisher, Alan W., 'Enlightened Despotism and Islam Under Catherine II', *Slavic Review*, vol. 27, no. 4, 1968, pp. 542–53

Flood, Finbarr B., *The Great Mosque of Damascus: Studies on the Makings of an Umayyad Visual Culture*, Leiden: Brill, 2001

Frinta, Mojmir S., 'The Frescoes from San Baudelio De Berlanga', *Gesta*, vol. 1/2, 1964, pp. 9–13

Garofalo, Vincenza, 'A Methodology for Studying Muqarnas: The Extant Examples in Palermo', *Muqarnas*, vol. 27, 2010, pp. 357–406

Ghazarian, Armen, and Robert Ousterhout, 'A Muqarnas Drawing from Thirteenth-Century Armenia and the Use of Architectural Drawings during the Middle Ages', *Muqarnas*, vol. 18, 2001, pp. 141–154

Giyasi, Jafar, 'Momina Khatun and Gudi Khatun Mausoleums in Nakhchivan', *IRS Heritage Journal*, vol. 3, no. 8, 2012

Golombek, Lisa, 'The So-Called "Turabeg Khanom" Mausoleum in Kunya Urgench: Problems of Attribution', *Muqarnas*, vol. 28, 2011, pp. 133–56

Gonella, Julia, 'Columns and Hieroglyphs: Magic "Spolia" in Medieval Islamic Architecture of Northern Syria', *Muqarnas*, vol. 27, 2010, pp. 103–20

González Pérez, Asunción, 'Las maquetas de la Alhambra en el siglo XIX: una fuente de difusión y de información acerca del conjunto Nazarí', PhD thesis, Universidad Autónoma de Madrid, 2017

Grabar, Oleg, 'From Dome of Heaven to Pleasure Dome', *Journal of the Society of Architectural Historians*, vol. 49, no. 1, 1990, pp. 15–21

Grabar, Oleg, and Renata Holod, 'A Tenth-Century Source for Architecture', *Harvard Ukrainian Studies*, vol. 3, no. 4, 1979, pp. 310–19

Gross, Jo-Ann, 'The Biographical Tradition of Mu ammad Bashārā: Sanctification and Legitimation in Tajikistan', in D. DeWeese and J. Gross, *Sufism in Central Asia*, Leiden; Boston: Brill, 2018, pp. 299–331

Gruber, C., 'The Missiri of Fréjus as healing memorial: mosque metaphors and the French colonial army (1928–64)', *International Journal of Islamic Architecture*, vol. 1, no. 1, 2012, pp. 25–60

Haddad, Elie, 'Between Myth and Reality: the "Tuscan influence" on the architecture of Mount Lebanon in the Emirate period', *Journal of Design History*, vol. 20, no. 2, 2007, pp. 161–71

Hallen, Barry, 'Afro-Brazilian Mosques in West Africa', *Mimar* 29, 1988, pp. 16–23

Harvey, L. P., 'The Mudejars', *The Legacy of Muslim Spain, Handbook of Oriental Studies* (2 vols), 2012, pp. 176–87

Herzfeld, Ernst, 'Damascus: Studies in Architecture: I', *Ars Islamica*, vol. 9, 1942, pp. 1–53

Hillenbrand, Robert, 'Turco-Iranian Elements in the Medieval Architecture of Pakistan: The Case of the Tomb of Rukn-I 'Alam at Multan', *Muqarnas*, vol. 9, no. 1, 1992, pp. 148–74

Holod, Renata, 'Text, Plan, and Building: On the Transmission of Architectural Knowledge' in Margaret Ševčenko (ed.), *Theories and Principles of Design in the Architecture of Islamic Societies*, Cambridge, MA: Aga Khan Program for Islamic Architecture, 1988, pp. 1–12

Isom-Verhaaren, Christine, 'Mihrimah Sultan: A Princess Constructs Ottoman Dynastic Identity' in K. F. Schull and C. Isom-Verhaaren, *Living in the Ottoman Realm: Empire and Identity, 13th to 20th Centuries*, Bloomington: Indiana University Press, 2016, pp. 152–53

Iwatake, Akio, 'The Waqf of a Timurid Amir', in N. Kondo, *Persian Documents: Social History of Iran and Turan in the 15th–19th Centuries*, Abingdon; New York: Routledge, 2004

Kana'an, R., 'Architectural Decoration in Islam: History and Techniques', in H. Selin, *Encyclopaedia of the History of Science, Technology, and Medicine in Non-Western Cultures*, Berlin; New York: Springer, 2008

Kaufmann, Katrin, 'The "Splendor of the Caliph's Dwellings" in Saint Petersburg. Aleksandr Briullov as a Pioneer of Neo-Moorish Style in Russia', *Art in Translation*, vol. 11, no. 2, 2019, pp. 181–99

Kaufmann, Thomas DaCosta, 'Islam, Art, and Architecture in the Americas: Some Considerations of Colonial Latin America', RES: *Anthropology and Aesthetics*, no. 43, 2003, pp. 42–50

Kaye, Maïra, 'The Material Culture and Architecture of the Jews of Central Asia. 1800–1920', MA thesis, University of Leiden, 2021

Koch, Ebba, *Mughal Architecture: An Outline of its History and Development* (1526–1858), Munich: Prestel, 1991

Koch, Ebba, 'The Taj Mahal: Architecture, Symbolism, and Urban Significance', *Muqarnas*, vol. 22, 2005, pp. 128–49

Kościelniak, Krzysztof, 'The Afaq (Apak) Khoja Mausoleum in Kashgar as a Symbol of Uyghur's Identity (ca 1640–2015)', *Analecta Cracoviensia* 49, 2017, pp. 249–81

Kösebay, Yonca, 'An Interpretive Analysis of Matrakçı Nasuh's Beyan-ı Menazil: Translating Text into Image', MS thesis, Massachusetts Institute of Technology, 1998

Ksiazek, Sarah, 'Architectural Culture in the Fifties: Louis Kahn and the National Assembly Complex in Dhaka', *Journal of the Society of Architectural Historians*, vol. 52, no. 4, 1993, pp. 416–35

Kuehn, S., 'The Dragon in Transcultural Skies: Its Celestial Aspect in the Medieval Islamic World', in N. Gutschow and K. Weiler (eds), *Spirits in Transcultural Skies*, Cham: Springer, 2015

Lambourn, Elizabeth, 'The Decoration of the Fakhr al-dīn Mosque in Mogadishu and Other Pieces of Gujarati Marble Carving on the East African Coast', AZANIA: *Journal of the British Institute in Eastern Africa*, vol. 34, no. 1, 1999, pp. 61–86

Lopez Gomez, Margarita, 'The Mozarabs: Worthy Bearers of Islamic Culture', *The Legacy of Muslim Spain, Handbook of Oriental Studies* (2 vols), 2012, pp. 171–75

López-Guzmán, Rafael, 'The Legacy of al-Andalus in Mexico: Mudejar Architecture', *Arts*, vol. 7, no. 30, 2018

Majeed, Tehnyat, 'The Role of the Qur'anic and Religious Inscriptions in the Buq'a Pīr-i Bakrān, Isfahan: The Shī'ī Reign of Öljeytü Khudābande in Īlkhānid Iran', *Journal of Qur'anic Studies*, vol. 10, no. 2, 2008, pp. 111–23

Markowitz, Fran, 'Tales of Two Buildings: National Entanglements in Sarajevo's Pasts, Presents and Futures', *Ethnologie Française*, vol. 42, no. 4, 2012, pp. 797–809

Mateo, Matilde, 'Breaking the Myth: Toledo Cathedral on the International Stage', *Journal of Art Historiography*, no. 17, 2017, pp. 1–30

Melville, C., 'New Light on Shah 'Abbas and the Construction of Isfahan', *Muqarnas*, vol. 33, 2016, pp. 155–76

Menocal, Maria Rosa, *The Ornament of the World: How Muslims, Jews and Christians Created a Culture of Tolerance in Medieval Spain*, New York: Little, Brown, 2003

Mernissi, Fatima, *The Forgotten Queens of Islam*, Cambridge: Polity Press, 1994

Michailidis, Melanie, 'Dynastic Politics and the Samanid Mausoleum', *Ars Orientalis* 44, pp. 20–39

Michelsen, Leslee and Stefan Masarovic, 'Collaborative Investigations of a Seljuq Stucco Panel', in S. Canby et al., *The Seljuqs and their Successors: Art, Culture and History*, Edinburgh: Edinburgh University Press, 2020

Morton, A. H., 'The Ardabīl Shrine in the Reign of Shāh Tahmāsp I', Iran, vol. 12, 1974, pp. 31–64

Mulder, Stephennie, 'The Mausoleum of Imam al-Shafi'i', Muqarnas, vol. 23, 2006, pp. 15–46

Njoto-Feillard, Hélène, 'Notes sur l'Identité des Modèles Architecturaux du Taman Sari de Yogyakarta (1758–1765)', 1st Congress of Réseau Asie-Asia Network, 24–25 September 2003, Paris, France

Northedge, Alastair, 'Creswell, Herzfeld, and Samarra', *Muqarnas*, vol. 8, 1991, pp. 74–93

O'Kane, Bernard, 'The Madrasa al-Ghiyāsīyya at Khargird', *Iran*, vol. 14, 1976, pp. 79–92

Özdural, Alpay, 'Omar Khayyam, Mathematicians, and "Conversazioni" with Artisans', *Journal of the Society of Architectural Historians*, vol. 54, no. 1, 1995, pp. 54–71

Özdural, Alpay, 'A Mathematical Sonata for Architecture: Omar Khayyam and the Friday Mosque of Isfahan', *Technology and Culture*, vol. 39, no. 4, 1998, pp. 699–715

Pancaroğlu, Oya, 'Devotion, Hospitality and Architecture in Medieval Anatolia', *Studia Islamica*, vol. 108, no. 1, 2013, pp. 48–81

Parodi, Laura E., '"The Distilled Essence of the Timurid Spirit": Some Observations on the Taj Mahal', East and West, vol. 50, no. 1/4, 2000, pp. 535–42

Paskaleva, Elena, 'The Bibi Khanum Mosque in Samarqand: Its Mongol and Timurid Architecture', The Silk Road 10, 2012, pp. 81–98

Pinder-Wilson, Ralph, 'Ghaznavid and Ghūrid Minarets', Iran, vol. 39, 2001, pp. 155–86

Polimeni, Beniamino, 'Describing a Unique Urban Culture: Ibadi Settlements of North

Africa', in F. Calabrò, L. Della Spina, C. Bevilacqua (eds), *International Symposium on New Metropolitan Perspectives*, Cham: Springer, 2018

Porter, Venetia Ann, 'The History and Monuments of the Tahirid dynasty of the Yemen, 858–923/1454–1517', PhD thesis, Durham University, 1992

Prevost, Virginie, 'Les mosquées ibadites du Maghreb', *Revue des mondes musulmans et de la Méditerranée* 125, 2009, pp. 217–32

Puertas, Antonio Fernández, 'I. Mezquita de Córdoba. Trazado Proporcional de su Planta General (Siglos VII–X)', *Archivo español de arte*, vol. 73, no. 291, 2000, pp. 217–47

Rabbat, Nasser, 'The Dome of the Rock Revisited: Some Remarks on al-Wasiti's Accounts', *Muqarnas*, vol. 10, 1993, pp. 67–75

Rabbat, Nasser, 'Al-Azhar Mosque: An Architectural Chronicle of Cairo's History', *Muqarnas*, vol. 13, 1996, pp. 45–67

Rabbat, Nasser, 'Design Without Representation in Medieval Egypt', *Muqarnas*, vol. 25, 2008, pp. 147–54

Rabbat, Nasser, 'The Pedigreed Domain of Architecture: A View from the Cultural Margin', *Perspecta*, vol. 44, 2011, pp. 6–11, 190–92

Raizman, David, 'The Church of Santa Cruz and the Beginnings of Mudejar Architecture in Toledo', *Gesta*, vol. 38, no. 2, 1999, pp. 128–41

Redford, Scott, 'The Seljuqs of Rum and the Antique', *Muqarnas*, vol. 10, 1993, pp. 148–56

Rogers, J. M., 'The Çifte Minare Medrese at Erzurum and the Gök Medrese at Sivas: A Contribution to the History of Style in the Seljuk Architecture of 13th Century Turkey', *Anatolian Studies*, vol. 15, 1965, pp. 63–85

Roxburgh, D. J., 'Ruy González De Clavijo's Narrative Of Courtly Life And Ceremony In Timur's Samarqand, 1404', in P. J. Brummett, *The 'Book' of Travels: Genre, Ethnology, and Pilgrimage, 1250–1700*, Leiden; Boston: Brill, 2009

Ruggles, D. Fairchild, 'The Alcazar of Seville and Mudejar Architecture', *Gesta*, vol. 43, no. 2, 2004, pp. 87–98

Ruggles, D. Fairchild, and Amita Sinha, 'Preserving the Cultural Landscape Heritage of Champaner-Pavagadh, Gujarat, India', in D. F. Ruggles and H. Silverman, *Intangible*

*Heritage Embodied*, New York: Springer, 2009, pp. 79–100

Sadek, Noha, 'In the Queen of Sheba's Footsteps: Women Patrons in Rasulid Yemen', Asian Art, vol. 6, no. 2, 1993

Savitri, Pradianti, Yohanes Purbadi and B. Sumardiyanto, 'Architectural Acculturation: Islamic and Javanese Spiritual Elements in Sumur Gumuling Design at Tamansari, Yogyakarta', *Jurnal Arsitektur Komposisi*, vol. 13, no. 2, 2020, pp. 73–85

Scherpe K. R., 'Reklame für Salem Aleikum', in A. Honold and K. R. Scherpe (eds), *Mit Deutschland um die Welt*, Stuttgart: J. B. Metzler, 2004, pp. 381–88

Sheren, I. N., 'Transcultured Architecture: Mudéjar's Epic Journey Reinterpreted', *Contemporaneity: Historical Presence in Visual Culture 1*, 2011, pp. 137–51

Sinclair, T. A., *Eastern Turkey: An Architectural and Archaeological Survey*, Volume IV, London: Pindar Press, 1990

Siry, Joseph M., 'Building as Bridge: Frank Lloyd Wright's Marin County Civic Center', *The Art Bulletin*, vol. 101, no. 3, 2019, pp. 115–45

Soucek, S., 'Timur and the Timurids' in S. Soucek, *A History of Inner Asia*, Cambridge: Cambridge University Press, 2000, pp. 123–43

Stegers, Rudolf, *Sacred Buildings: A Design Manual*, Basel; Boston; Berlin: Birkhäuser, 2008

Steinhardt, Nancy Shatzman, 'China's Earliest Mosques', *Journal of the Society of Architectural Historians*, vol. 67, no. 3, 2008, pp. 330–61

Subtelny, M. E., 'A Timurid Educational and Charitable Foundation: The Ikhlāsiyya Complex of 'Alī Shīr Navā'ī in 15th-Century Herat and Its Endowment', *Journal of the American Oriental Society*, vol. 111, no. 1, 1991, p. 38

Tabbaa, Yasser, *Constructions of Power and Piety in Medieval Aleppo*, University Park: Pennsylvania State Press, 2010

Wakelnig, Elvira, 'Socrates in the Arabic Tradition: An Esteemed Monotheist with Moist Blue Eyes', in C. Moore, *Brill's Companion to the Reception of Socrates*, Leiden; Boston: Brill, 2019

Waldron, Lawrence, 'Ephemeral Architecture: The Fleeting Forms of West African Adobe Mosques', *Architecture Caribbean* online, 2011

# Picture Credits

123superstar/123RF.COM 31a; A. Tamboly/Westend61 GmbH/Alamy Stock Photo 292; AFP via Getty Images 59; Ahmet Kuş/Alamy Stock Photo 160; Albaraa Mansoor 57; Aleksandar Pavlovic/Dreamstime.com 96a, 98a; Alexander Moskovskiy/Alamy Stock Photo 279b; Aliraza Khatri's Photography/Moment/Getty Images 96b; Allison Bailey/Alamy Stock Photo 44-45; Amir Mohtasemi Ltd 267b; Amitabha Gupta 91a; Amors photos/Shutterstock 128a; Andreas Zerndl/Shutterstock 271a; Antoine Boureau/Photononstop/Getty Images 163; Anton Ivanov/Alamy Stock Photo 76-77; Anton_Ivanov/Shutterstock 78b; Antonella865/Dreamstime.com 156b; Arlo K. Abrahamson/PJF Military Collection/Alamy Stock Photo 69a; Avishek Das/SOPA Images/LightRocket via Getty Images 95b; Ayhan Iscen/Anadolu Agency/Getty Images 136; Azim Khan Ronnie/awl-images.com 108-109; B.O'Kane/Alamy Stock Photo 13, 17, 18, 32a, 32b, 34, 72a, 72b, 79, 81, 82-83, 84b, 116, 121al, 133, 140, 157, 189, 212, 298b, 311; Bashar Shglila/Moment/Getty Images 191b; Bashar Tabbah 47b, 48-49, 184a; Bashir Osman's Photography/Moment Unreleased/Getty Images 101; BE&W agencja; fotograficzna Sp. z o.o./Alamy Stock Photo 295; Ben Johnson/Arcaid Images/Alamy Stock Photo 286; Bertrand Rieger/Hemis/Alamy Stock Photo 285, 300-301; Bjorn Holland/Photodisc/Getty Images 156a; bokehcambodia/Alamy Stock Photo 224; Boris Kester/traveladventures.org 199a; Brasilnut/Dreamstime.com 73; Brian Overcast/Alamy Stock Photo 249; Britta Franke/Dreamstime.com 208; C. Sappa/DeAgostini/Getty Images 69b; Catharina Lux/mauritius images GmbH/Alamy Stock Photo 177; Cheryl Rinzler/Alamy Stock Photo 176b; Christian Heeb/awl-images.com 168; Christophe Boisvieux/agefotostock 98b, 100; Christophe Boisvieux/Corbis/Getty Images 110; Chrysovalantis Lamprianidis/The Museum of Islamic Art, Doha 65; Cihan Demirci/Anadolu Agency/Getty Images 126-127; Clive Gracey/clivegracey.net 54; Cortyn/Shutterstock 188; Courtesy Ogasawara Hakushaku Tei, Tokyo 237; Dallet-Alba/Alamy Stock Photo 4l, 20b, 42; Dani Friedman/vario Images RM/agefotostock 308; Daniel Prudek/Alamy Stock Photo 162a; Danko Stjepanovic, courtesy Sharjah Art Foundation 22; Dave Stamboulis/Alamy Stock Photo 104a; Davor Curic/Moment Open/Getty Images 293; dbtravel/Alamy Stock Photo 75b; Dick

Osseman 122a; Dinodia Photos/Alamy Stock Photo 92; Dr Ajay Kumar Singh/Shutterstock 93a; Eddie Gerald/Alamy Stock Photo 46b, 158-159; Edmund Sumner 55a; Education Images/Universal Images Group North America LLC/Alamy Stock Photo 303a; Emad Aljumah/Getty Images 252b; Emanuele Vidal/ClickAlps/awl-images.com 256; EmmePi Travel/Alamy Stock Photo 272a; Eric Lafforgue/Alamy Stock Photo 172-173, 190, 199b, 200, 204; Estan Cabigas/Alamy Stock Photo 5c, 225, 226-227; Evgeniy Fesenko/Dreamstime.com 29a, 36-37, 87b, 183; Fabio Lamanna/Dreamstime.com 88b; Falkensteinfoto/Alamy Stock Photo 121b; Fatima Muhammad-Amusa 209; Fatma Jamal 33; FB-Fischer/imageBROKER/Alamy Stock Photo 4c, 103; Felix Lipov/Alamy Stock Photo 4r; Fine Art Images/Heritage Image Partnership Ltd/Alamy Stock Photo 315; Focus and Blur/Shutterstock 68b; Fotystory/Shutterstock 82; Franck Guiziou/Hemis/Alamy Stock Photo 90; Frans Sellies/Moment/Getty Images 63; funkyfood London - Paul Williams/Alamy Stock Photo 129, 180, 273; Gary Otte 162b; Gavin Hellier/awl-images.com 21; Gerard Degeorge/akg-images 89b, 93b; Ghigo Roli/Bridgeman Images 272b; Giuseppe Spartà/Alamy Stock Photo 250-251; Gordon Sinclair/Alamy Stock Photo 184b; Grant Rooney Premium/Alamy Stock Photo 145; Hakan Can Yalcin/Dreamstime.com 78a; Hasan Zaidi/Dreamstime.com 51; Hervé Lenain/Alamy Stock Photo 288; Hikrcn/Dreamstime.com 27; Hoberman Collection/Hoberman Publishing/Alamy Stock Photo 12; Hufton+Crow/View Pictures/Universal Images Group via Getty Images 14; Huib Blom/Alamy Stock Photo 194a; Ildar Davletshin/Dreamstime.com 280; Images & Stories/Alamy Stock Photo 5l, 70-71, 170-171; Isa Özdere/Alamy Stock Photo 137; iStock.com/Drazen_ 228-229; iStock.com/EgyptianStudio 30b; iStock.com/fokkebok 232-233; iStock.com/LeoPatrizi 125a; iStock.com/mazzzur 80; iStock.com/Mediattivo 265; iStock.com/mtcurado 156c, 198a, 198b, 202; iStock.com/Nikada 220; iStock.com/okanmetin 124a; iStock.com/serkansenturk 40b; iStock.com/Thomas Markert 196-197; iStock.com/usas 119c; iStock.com/Vladimir Zapletin 281; iStock.com/vuk8691 107; iStock.com/Zastavkin 130-131; Ivan Sebborn/Alamy Stock Photo 31b; Ivan Vdovin/Alamy Stock Photo 19, 216; Ivan Vdovin/Jon Arnold Images Ltd/Alamy Stock Photo 28, 147, 161b; Iwan

Baan 106; Izzet Keribar/Getty Images 120a; J.D. Dallet/agefotostock/Alamy Stock Photo 38; James Wang, courtesy studio chahar 195; Javier Ayarza 261b; Jean-Pierre Degas/Hemis/Alamy Stock Photo 266; Jess Kraft/Shutterstock 310; jessmine/123RF.COM 24-25; Joe Daniel Price/Moment Open/Getty Images 304a; John Copland/Shutterstock 179; John Gollings 238; Jon Chica/Shutterstock 178; Jonathan Wilson/Dreamstime.com 152b; Jono Photography/Shutterstock 152a, 153; José Antonio Sanz Martín/Dreamstime.com 261a; Juanma Aparicio/Alamy Stock Photo 262; Juergen Ritterbach/Alamy Stock Photo 2, 30a, 141; Kadagan/Shutterstock 138-139; Karen Brodie/Moment Mobile/Getty Images 309; Karl F. Schöfmann/imageBROKER/Alamy Stock Photo 124b; Karol Kozlowski/robertharding/Alamy Stock Photo 23a; Keren Su/China Span/Alamy Stock Photo 165; Kerstin Bittner/Westend61 GmbH/Alamy Stock Photo 290a; Khaled ElAdawy/Alamy Stock Photo 125b; Khaled Fazaa/AFP via Getty Images 56; L. Romano/Universal Images Group North America LLC/DeAgostini/Alamy Stock Photo 271b; Len4foto/Dreamstime.com 236; Library of Congress, Washington, D.C., Prints & Photographs Division, photograph by Carol M. Highsmith [Reproduction No. LC-DIG-highsm-28791] 305; Lindman Photography 278; Lisa S. Engelbrecht/Danita Delimont/Alamy Stock Photo 270a; Liz Coughlan/Alamy Stock Photo 275; Luc Boegly/Artedia/Bridgeman Images 5r, 303b; Lucas Vallecillos/Alamy Stock Photo 181, 185; Maleficeliya/Dreamstime.com 296; Mapache/Shutterstock 113; Mark Luscombe-Whyte 132; Mark Sykes/awl-images.com 282; Martin Sasse/DuMont Bildarchiv/dpa picture alliance/Alamy Stock Photo 20a; Martin Siepmann/imageBROKER/Alamy Stock Photo 134-135; Martin Siepmann/Westend61 GmbH/Alamy Stock Photo 119b; Mary F. Calvert/ZUMA Press, Inc./Alamy Stock Photo 210-211; Matthew Millman 302; Matyas Rehak/Dreamstime.com 164; Mauricio Abreu/awl-images.com 150; Max Milligan/awl-images.com 206-207; MehmetO/Alamy Stock Photo 117a, 122b; Metropolitan Museum of Art, New York. Mr. and Mrs. Isaac D. Fletcher Collection, Bequest of Isaac D. Fletcher and Rogers Fund, by exchange, 1985, Accession No. 1985.241 174b; Michael Runkel/imageBROKER/Alamy Stock Photo 68a, 194b; Michael Runkel/robertharding/Alamy Stock Photo 67; Michael von Aichberger/Alamy

Stock Photo 291a; Michael Wald/Alamy Stock Photo 304b; Michele Falzone/Alamy Stock Photo 43a; Mobeen Ansari 97; Mohammed Younos/Shutterstock 26; Mr NongKhai/Shutterstock 234; Muhammad Mostafigur Rahman/Alamy Stock Photo 104b; Muhammed Kösen 114-115; Murat Taner/Photodisc/Getty Images 123; Nadeem Khawar/Moment Open/Getty Images 99; Nadeem Khawar/Moment/Getty Images 102; Naquib Hossain/dotproduct.ca 105; Niels Poulsen/Alamy Stock Photo 299b; Nigel Pavitt/John Warburton-Lee Photography/Alamy Stock Photo 192-193; Nik Wheeler/Alamy Stock Photo 240; Nikolai Sorokin/Dreamstime.com 119a; Nizar Kauzar/Shutterstock 222-223; Nöstler Photo 299a; Oliver Gerhard/imageBROKER/Alamy Stock Photo 39, 41; Olivier Bourgeois/Alamy Stock Photo 40a; Omair Aleem/Makhzan-e-Tasaweer Image Library 297; Orhan Durgut/Alamy Stock Photo 47a; Oronoz/Album/Alamy Stock Photo 253; ozgur_oral/Shutterstock 128b; PantherMediaSeller/Depositphotos.com 43b; Patrick Foto/Shutterstock 230a; Patrizia Wyss/Alamy Stock Photo 75a; Paul M.R. Maeyaert/Bildarchiv Monheim GmbH/Alamy Stock Photo 270b; Paul Melling/Alamy Stock Photo 64; Peter Eastland/Alamy Stock Photo 252a; Peter Fischer/awl-images.com 176a; Peter Horree/Alamy Stock Photo 66; Petrajz/Dreamstime.com 318-319; Philip Lee Harvey 10; Philippe Lissac/The Image Bank Unreleased/Getty Images 203; Pictures from History/CPA Media Pte Ltd/Alamy Stock Photo 144; Prisma Archivo/Alamy Stock Photo 16, 46a; Rachel Carbonell/Alamy Stock Photo 6; Rafael Santos Rodriguez/Alamy Stock Photo 269; Raga Jose Fuste/Prisma by Dukas Presseagentur GmbH/Alamy Stock Photo 267a; Raimund Franken/imageBROKER/Alamy Stock Photo 120b; Raimund Franken/ullstein bild via Getty Images 85a, 85b; Rangzen/Dreamstime.com 230b; raspu/Moment Open/Getty Images 175; Razak.R/Shutterstock 84a; Reflex Life/Shutterstock 276-277; Ricardo Bofill Taller de Arquitectura 191a; Risqi Zed/Dreamstime.com 221; Robert Nawrocki/Dreamstime.com 58; Robert Wyatt/Alamy Stock Photo 148-149, 161a; Roland and Sabrina Michaud/akg-images 121ar, 241, 321; Romain Cintract/Hemis/Alamy Stock Photo 289a; Sammlung; Rauch/Interfoto/Alamy Stock Photo 291b; Sarah Bray/Shutterstock 274; scaliger/123RF.COM 283; sedmak/123RF.COM 264; Serjo_Serjo/Shutterstock 166-167; Serkan Senturk/ZUMA Press Wire/Alamy Stock Photo 117b; Shalini Saran/IndiaPicture/Alamy Stock Photo 316; Shaun Egan/The Image Bank/Getty Images 263; Sir Cam 298a; Sketchh/Shutterstock 95a; Sophie James/Shutterstock 242; Stefan Auth/imageBROKER/Alamy Stock Photo 174a; Stefano Politi Markovina/Alamy Stock Photo 50, 246; Stefano Politi Markovina/awl-images.com 235; Stefano Politi Markovina/Jon Arnold Images Ltd/Alamy Stock Photo 257; Steve Outram/Aurora Photos/Cavan Images/Alamy Stock Photo 201; Suzuki Kaku/Alamy Stock Photo 29b; Tammy Gaber 239; Tanarch/Shutterstock 94; Bildarchiv Foto Marburg/Bayerische Schlösserverwaltung/Rose Hajdu 290b; Teo Krijgsman 289b; Tesnim Karišik Spahić 294a; The Picture Art Collection/Alamy Stock Photo 86a; Thierry Falise/LightRocket via Getty Images 231; Tibor Bognar/Alamy Stock Photo 52-53; TMI/Alamy Stock Photo 88a; Tom Schulze/DuMont Bildarchiv/dpa picture alliance/Alamy Stock Photo 74; Tomka/Alamy Stock Photo 254-255; Ton Koene/Alamy Stock Photo 154-155; Toniflap/Alamy Stock Photo 112; Toño Labra/agefotostock/Alamy Stock Photo 35; Torbenbrinker 214-215; Touseef designer/Shutterstock 23b; Travel Guy/Alamy Stock Photo 89a; travel4pictures/Alamy Stock Photo 151; TravelCollection/Image Professionals GmbH/Alamy Stock Photo 60; TravelMuse/Alamy Stock Photo 218-219; Tuul & Bruno Morandi/The Image Bank/Getty Images 312-313; Tuul and Bruno Morandi/Alamy Stock Photo 55b, 86b, 91b, 146; UlyssePixel/Alamy Stock Photo 142-143; Underwood Archives/Getty Images 306-307; V4ID Afsahi/Alamy Stock Photo 87a; Valery Egorov/Shutterstock 268; Viennaslide/Construction Photography/Avalon/Hulton Archive/Getty Images 287; Walter Bibikow/Jon Arnold Images Ltd/Alamy Stock Photo 284; Werner Forman/Heritage Image Partnership Ltd/Alamy Stock Photo 186-187, 259; Weston Westmoreland 260; Will Perrett/Alamy Stock Photo 258; Xavier Rossi/Gamma-Rapho via Getty Images 205; Yakov Oskanov/Alamy Stock Photo 118; Yann Jouanique/Alamy Stock Photo 244-255; Yulia Babkina/Alamy Stock Photo 279a; Yunus Demirbas/Anadolu Agency/Getty Images 294b; Zhang Peng/LightRocket via Getty Images 243

# Index

Page references in *italic* refer to illustrations

## Author's Acknowledgments

A book like this is a team effort. I'd like to first thank Philip, Aaron and Amanda at Thames & Hudson for the opportunity to make another beautiful book together. A grateful thank you to Angelika Pirkl and Tahir Iqbal for bringing the visuals to life and to Kirsty Seymour-Ure for making all my words fit. A special thanks to all the photographers I reached out to in my search for the best photos. I wrote this book during the COVID pandemic. Only my wife and daughter, Kalwa and Andrea, know the extent to which this book project consumed me for two years. Without their presence and support, there would be no book.

I'd like to express my gratitude for the help and support I received from:
Razwan Baig, Madiha Bakir, Abdelkader Benali, Hamza Bermejo,
Philipp Bruckmayr, Haris Dervisevic, Robert Hillenbrand, Hashim Khalifa,
Ehab Mokhtar, Yusra al-Nakeeb, Nasir Noormohamed, Susan Parker-Leavy,
Beniamino Polimeni, Shahed Saleem, Ali Reza Sarvdalir, Sultan al Qassemi,
Ahmed Bin Shabib, Mansoure Shahi, Laila Sharif, Hadeed Ahmed Sher
and Nancy S. Steinhardt.

First published in the United Kingdom in 2023 by
Thames & Hudson Ltd, 181A High Holborn, London WC1V 7QX

First published in the United States of America in 2023 by
Thames & Hudson Inc., 500 Fifth Avenue, New York, New York 10110

*Islamic Architecture: A World History* © 2023 Thames & Hudson Ltd, London

Text © 2023 Eric Broug

Designed by Tahir Iqbal

British Library Cataloguing-in-Publication Data
A catalogue record for this book is available from the British Library

Library of Congress Control Number 2023933205

ISBN 978-0-500-34378-4

Printed and bound in China by C & C Offset Printing Co. Ltd

Be the first to know about our new releases,
exclusive content and author events by visiting
**thamesandhudson.com**
**thamesandhudsonusa.com**
**thamesandhudson.com.au**